The 30-Minute COOKING —FROM— FROZEN Cookbook

100 Delicious Recipes That Will Save You Time and Money— No Pre-Thawing Required!

CAROLE JONES OF MYKITCHENESCAPADES.COM

Adams Media

New York   London   Toronto   Sydney   New Delhi

Aadamsmedia

Adams Media
An Imprint of Simon & Schuster, Inc.
57 Littlefield Street
Avon, Massachusetts 02322

First Adams Media trade paperback edition October 2020

ADAMS MEDIA and colophon are trademarks of Simon & Schuster.

For information about special discounts for bulk purchases, please contact Simon & Schuster Special Sales at 1-866-506-1949 or business@simonandschuster.com.

The Simon & Schuster Speakers Bureau can bring authors to your live event. For more information or to book an event contact the Simon & Schuster Speakers Bureau at 1-866-248-3049 or visit our website at www.simonspeakers.com.

Interior design by Julia Jacintho
Interior photographs by James Stefiuk

Manufactured in the United States of America

10 9 8 7 6 5 4 3 2 1

Library of Congress Cataloging-in-Publication Data
Names: Jones, Carole (Food blogger), author.
Title: The 30-minute cooking from frozen cookbook / Carole Jones of MyKitchenEscapades.com.
Description: Avon, Massachusetts: Adams Media, 2020. | Includes index.
Identifiers: LCCN 2020017469 | ISBN 9781507214183 (pb) | ISBN 9781507214190 (ebook)
Subjects: LCSH: Cooking (Frozen foods) | Frozen foods. | LCGFT: Cookbooks.
Classification: LCC TX828 .J66 2020 | DDC 641.6/153--dc23
LC record available at https://lccn.loc.gov/2020017469

ISBN 978-1-5072-1418-3
ISBN 978-1-5072-1419-0 (ebook)

Contents

Chapter Three

SIDE DISHES......45

Chapter Four

CHICKEN MAIN DISHES......67

Chapter Five
BEEF AND PORK MAIN DISHES......91

Chapter Six

FISH AND SEAFOOD MAIN DISHES......115

Chapter Seven

VEGETARIAN MAIN DISHES......139

Chapter Eight
DESSERT RECIPES......161

US/Metric Conversion Chart 183

Index 185

Introduction

Want to get a healthy and delicious meal on the table quickly? Check your freezer!

Today, the frozen food section at your local grocery store features so much more than premade meals in plastic containers. You can find grilled zucchini strips, sticky white rice, crushed fresh garlic, cooked meats, cauliflower pizza crust, and spiraled vegetables, just to name a few. This plethora of frozen ingredients is an amazing resource for getting dinner on the table in 30 minutes or less.

There are so many benefits of using frozen ingredients in cooking. Frozen foods enjoy a long shelf life—no more moldy produce or slimy proteins. Plus, frozen foods provide affordable, year-round access to ingredients and produce that might otherwise be seasonal. Some produce is also less expensive when purchased frozen (since it is frozen close to the source at the peak of freshness, there is no waste or spoilage and companies can pass on that savings to you!).

Another great benefit of the recipes in this cookbook is that you can use the frozen ingredients as is—no need to allow for time to thaw them in the refrigerator! Just pull your culinary inspiration straight out of the freezer, use as instructed in the recipe, and *voilà*! You've got a mouthwatering dish finished in half an hour.

Throughout this book, I will also teach you tips and tricks that will make working with frozen foods simple and easy. (In other words, you'll be able to avoid watery vegetables, mushy fruit, and rubbery shrimp!) You'll also learn how to stock your pantry so you're ready to make a variety of meals at a moment's notice. You will get the same impressive results using frozen ingredients as you would using fresh.

Whether you're looking to start your day off right (try Lemon Poppy Seed Pancakes with Mixed Berry Compote), make a family-favorite weeknight meal (such as Cheesy Ground Beef Nacho Casserole), add a quick side dish (maybe the tasty Parmesan Garlic–Roasted Brussels Sprouts), or finish off with a sweet treat (don't miss the Peach Pie Roll-Ups), this book has recipes sure to please any palate. Create dozens of delicious meals in 30 minutes or less—thanks to your freezer!

Chapter One

COOKING WITH FROZEN INGREDIENTS

MANY PEOPLE ONLY THINK OF THE FROZEN FOOD AISLES WHEN THEY WANT TO GRAB A QUICK PREMADE MEAL OR SOME ICE CREAM—BUT THERE ARE COUNTLESS TREASURES AVAILABLE THERE NOWADAYS. DELICIOUS OUT-OF-SEASON BERRIES, PRECHOPPED VEGGIES, COOKED MEATS—YOU CAN FIND DOZENS OF OPTIONS THAT WILL MAKE YOUR MEAL PREP EASIER AND FASTER. WORKING WITH FROZEN INGREDIENTS IS A LITTLE DIFFERENT FROM COOKING WITH FRESH, BUT THIS CHAPTER WILL OUTLINE ALL THE KEY INFORMATION YOU NEED TO GET STARTED. ONCE YOU KNOW HOW TO USE FROZEN FOODS PROPERLY, YOU WILL NEVER BE ABLE TO TELL THE DIFFERENCE BETWEEN FROZEN AND FRESH. READ ON TO LEARN SOME TIPS AND TRICKS THAT WILL MAKE COOKING FROM FROZEN A SNAP.

GO EXPLORING

The next time you have a few extra moments to spare at your local grocery store, spend some time seeing what's available in the frozen food aisles. You can skip the sections with prepared dinners and pizzas and focus on all the individual ingredients at your fingertips. It will be eye opening! Once you have a better understanding of what is there, you can make the one hundred recipes in this book and figure out how to use those ingredients on your own. You will begin to see how you can make your grandma's famous Praline Sweet Potatoes recipe in half the time, and without losing any flavor...or how you can find the fruit you like for smoothies when it's out of season.

When selecting which frozen produce to purchase, always pick a bag over a box if you have a choice. The bag allows you to easily scoop out the needed amount right from the freezer. Those frozen bricks of produce may be a bit cheaper, but they aren't worth the money savings if you end up wasting a bunch of it because you only need a small amount at a time. Plus, there are a few recipes where you will need to cook the produce in the microwave, and freezer bags are all microwave safe and vent out the steam perfectly.

THE BENEFITS OF COOKING FROM FROZEN

There are so many reasons to try cooking from frozen ingredients. For example, you'll:

- **Save time:** When using frozen ingredients in recipes, all the washing, trimming, and chopping has already been done for you. That is a massive time saver in any recipe! All you need to do is open a bag and add it in.

- **Eliminate hassle:** If you are feeling hesitant to try frozen ingredients, start with one product in particular: frozen chopped onions. Once you experience how much easier frozen onions are to deal with (no more watery eyes!), it will give you confidence to try more.
- **Save money:** Frozen foods often cost less than fresh. For example, a bag of frozen chopped onions usually costs less than a dollar and lasts for months. The current average price of fresh cauliflower florets is $3.13 per pound, but you can get that same pound of cauliflower florets for about $1.75 per pound in the freezer section.

THE HIGH NUTRITIONAL VALUE OF FROZEN PRODUCE

Frozen fruits and vegetables often get a bad rap for being less nutritious or less fresh. That is false. The fact is that fresh produce loses nutrients from the time it is picked until it is served at your table. It may be weeks before fresh fruits and veggies even land in your refrigerator, let alone on your table.

Produce that is frozen, on the other hand, is usually processed within hours of being picked. The nutrients are then contained in that fruit or vegetable. Freezing has no effect on the fiber content either! As an example, both frozen peas and frozen spinach contain more vitamin C than their fresh counterparts. Those peas and spinach lose 50 percent of their vitamin C within the first 48 hours of harvesting.

HOW TO AVOID SOGGY FOOD

Cooking with frozen ingredients does not have to lead to soggy, mushy foods! Yes, frozen food does have a higher moisture content that needs to be managed appropriately. Here are two key ways to do that:

1. Whether you are cooking in the oven or on the stovetop, use high heat.

2. Preheat your pan or oven.

When you're in a hurry, it's tempting to skip the preheating step—but when cooking with frozen ingredients, it's very important. When you toss those frozen veggies into a hot pan on the stovetop, that excess moisture will quickly evaporate and your veggies will sauté and brown. If you toss them into a partially warmed pan, they will slowly release their moisture and steam instead of sauté. That is how you end up with mushy vegetables.

When cooking in the oven, again, high heat is key. Did you know you can roast frozen vegetables in the oven just like you can fresh? When you use high heat, they turn out perfectly caramelized on the outside despite their need to release that excess moisture. Pay attention to that temperature setting and allow the oven to fully preheat before cooking. Don't let the higher oven temperatures of many of these recipes intimidate you. Most of us are used to a moderate 350°F, but the recipes in this book will be in the 400°F–450°F range. You won't burn the food—you will make perfectly oven-roasted meals.

DOUBLING RECIPES

When you want to double a recipe that uses frozen ingredients, you'll need to adjust your pan size more than usual. When cooking anything frozen in a sauté pan, adding too many of those cold ingredients crowded together in a small pan will create a pool of water. You need a bit of space in the pan for the water to escape and evaporate. If you want to double a recipe, just do so separately in a second pan, baking sheet, or skillet.

THERE'S NO NEED TO THAW EVERYTHING FIRST!

It will be tempting to "save some time" by putting the frozen ingredients in the fridge ahead of time so that they are already thawed when you want to use them. Resist this urge! Many of the frozen products in the recipes in this book are meant to be used straight from the freezer. If you allow your bag of frozen peaches to thaw in the fridge before making Peach Pie Roll-Ups, you will end up with mushy, overcooked peaches in your finished product instead of peaches that have just enough firmness and texture in every bite.

If a particular ingredient does need to be thawed before you use it, it will take only a few minutes in the microwave, so don't do it ahead of time in the fridge. You'll see those instructions in the recipes; trust them.

This no-thaw point is especially important when using frozen fish fillets. I promise, they will go from frozen rock hard to perfectly tender and flaky without ever needing to thaw. Granted, it will feel a bit odd to you to rub seasonings and spices into a frozen fish fillet, but it works wonderfully.

Remember to keep foods frozen if you have long trips home from the grocery store too. If you own some of those amazing freezer bags, keep them in your car so you have them whenever you need them. Then pack all your frozen ingredients together in these bags (or ask the bagger to do so). If you don't own freezer bags, just keep a couple of blankets in your trunk. You can wrap the bags of frozen food in those blankets, and they will act as an insulator to keep everything cold.

There are two main reasons you don't want items to thaw, even partially, on the way home:

1. **The texture can change:** First off, it messes with the texture of your food if it has thawed and then refrozen. For example, have you ever had ice cream that was a bit icier throughout than normal? That happened because somewhere along the production and shipping process, it partially thawed and was refrozen.

2. **Ice crystals can form:** The second argument for a cold ride home is that the thaw-freeze cycle will create large ice crystals all over the surface of your food, increasing the chances for freezer burn and loss of flavor. Plus, no one likes those big blocks of frozen food that happen as a result. You know, those bags of frozen peas that you have to smash over and over again on the counter before using them? You want to keep the individual pieces of frozen ingredients in each container exactly that—individual.

GETTING STARTED

Now that you have some background information, it's time to start cooking. Each of the following one hundred recipes uses the frozen ingredients in many different ways. My hope is that after being exposed to different cooking methods, you will gain confidence to try using frozen food on your own. For example, after a few recipes you will learn how frozen onions and garlic behave in a hot pan so you will be able to adapt your own personal recipes. Go forth and learn how to become a master in cooking with frozen foods, then share that knowledge with the world around you. Your friends and family are just as short on time as you are and will welcome your tips!

Chapter Two

BREAKFAST RECIPES

NO MATTER HOW BLEARY-EYED YOU FEEL IN THE MORNING, A GREAT BREAKFAST WILL HELP YOU FEEL ENERGIZED AND KICK OFF A SUCCESSFUL DAY. DO YOUR BRAIN AND BODY A FAVOR BY FEEDING THEM WELL EVERY MORNING. WHILE COLD CEREAL AND DRY TOAST ARE EASY OPTIONS, THEY AREN'T SATISFYING AND HEARTY ENOUGH TO KEEP YOU GOING STRONG UNTIL LUNCHTIME. THIS CHAPTER CONTAINS MANY DIFFERENT CHOICES, DEPENDING ON HOW MUCH TIME YOU HAVE AND WHAT YOU ARE CRAVING. YOU'LL FIND EVERYTHING FROM A QUICK, HEALTHY BOWL OF OAT-MEAL TO PANCAKES MADE FROM SCRATCH.

SOME OF THESE MORNING RECIPES WORK GREAT AS A BREAKFAST ON THE GO, BUT THE REAL BEAUTY OF THE FIRST MEAL OF THE DAY CAN BE FOUND ON A QUI-ETER WEEKEND MORNING. CELEBRATE YOUR DAY OFF FROM WORK AND SCHOOL WITH A REAL BREAKFAST TOGETHER AS A FAMILY. GET YOUR LOVED ONES IN THE KITCHEN WITH YOU AND CREATE SOME MEMORIES COOKING TOGETHER BEFORE DEVOURING ALL YOUR HARD WORK. THAT IS HOW YOU KICK OFF A PERFECT FAMILY WEEKEND!

TROPICAL MANGO GREEN SMOOTHIE

A healthy breakfast on the go in 3 minutes flat is a great idea for your busiest mornings! Green smoothies are a delicious way to sneak a few more healthy greens into your daily diet. If you want a bit more protein, a couple of tablespoons of chia or flax seeds make a great addition. This recipe works best made in individual batches, as written, so your blender doesn't get bogged down with too many ingredients at once.

SERVES: 1
PREP TIME: 3 minutes
COOK TIME: N/A
TOTAL TIME: 3 minutes

Ingredients

½ cup unsweetened coconut almond milk

½ cup frozen chopped spinach

1 medium seedless orange, peeled and sectioned

½ cup frozen sliced peaches

½ cup frozen chopped mango

½ cup frozen chopped pineapple

PER SERVING

Calories: 226
Fat: 2g
Protein: 6g
Sodium: 117mg

Fiber: 10g
Carbohydrates: 51g
Sugar: 39g

1. In the pitcher of a blender, add almond milk, spinach, and orange sections. Process on high until smooth.

2. With the blender running on high, add pieces of frozen peaches, mango, and pineapple one at a time. Blend until smooth. Serve immediately.

PEACH COBBLER OATMEAL

These loaded oatmeal bowls are deliciously addictive and done in 5 minutes. While this recipe tastes indulgent with the use of peaches, brown sugar, and almonds, each bowl is less than 300 calories. For best results and the freshest texture, make each bowl individually as opposed to making one large batch for everyone. Hey, they only take 2 minutes each in the microwave, so it couldn't be simpler!

SERVES: 1
PREP TIME: 8 minutes
COOK TIME: 7 minutes
TOTAL TIME: 15 minutes

Ingredients

2 teaspoons slivered almonds

½ cup old-fashioned rolled oats

½ cup water

⅛ teaspoon kosher salt

½ cup frozen sliced peaches

¼ cup 1% milk

1 tablespoon brown sugar

⅛ teaspoon cinnamon

⅛ teaspoon vanilla extract

PER SERVING

Calories: 284
Fat: 6g
Protein: 9g
Sodium: 319mg

Fiber: 6g
Carbohydrates: 52g
Sugar: 24g

1. In a small skillet over medium-high heat, toast almonds for 5 minutes until golden brown, stirring often. Remove from heat and set aside.

2. In a small microwave-safe bowl, combine oats, water, salt, and peaches. Microwave on high for 2 minutes.

3. Remove and use spoon to cut peaches into bite-sized pieces. Add milk, brown sugar, almonds, cinnamon, and vanilla. Mix well and serve immediately.

TATER TOT BREAKFAST STACKERS

The surprising key to quick and crispy breakfast potatoes is your waffle iron. These "waffles" are perfectly crunchy and make a delightful base for this breakfast tower. Personalize this recipe however you feel inspired. Use ham or bacon instead of sausage, or swap out the spinach for onions, mushrooms, kale, or asparagus, all of which you can find in the freezer section of your grocery store. The hollandaise sauce pulls all the flavors together and cooks in less than 30 seconds in the microwave!

SERVES: 4
PREP TIME: 8 minutes
COOK TIME: 7 minutes
TOTAL TIME: 15 minutes

Stackers

35 frozen Tater Tots (about ⅓ of a 2-pound bag)

1 cup frozen chopped spinach

4 precooked frozen sausage patties

4 large eggs

¼ teaspoon kosher salt

¼ teaspoon ground black pepper

Microwave Hollandaise Sauce

2 large egg yolks

½ teaspoon lemon juice

⅛ teaspoon kosher salt

⅛ teaspoon ground cayenne pepper

4 tablespoons salted butter, melted

TATER TOT BREAKFAST STACKERS CONT.

1. Preheat waffle iron to high. Lightly grease with nonstick spray.

2. To make the stackers, thaw Tater Tots in the microwave on high for 1–2 minutes. Cover the surface of waffle iron with tots, squeeze down the lid, and cook until crispy, about 6–7 minutes. Remove from waffle iron and cut "waffle" into four sections. Set aside.

3. While tots cook, in a small microwave-safe bowl, microwave spinach on high for 2 minutes. Remove and drain spinach in mesh strainer lined with a double layer of paper towels. Remove as much water as possible by squeezing spinach inside the paper towels until it stops dripping. Set aside.

4. Heat sausage patties in microwave according to package directions. Set aside.

5. Heat a large skillet over high heat and lightly grease with nonstick spray. Crack eggs into hot pan, sprinkle on salt and pepper, and cook until edges begin to brown, about 2 minutes. Flip and cook another minute. Set aside.

6. To make the hollandaise sauce, in a small microwave-safe bowl, whisk together egg yolks, lemon juice, salt, and cayenne. While whisking, slowly drizzle in melted butter. Microwave on high in two 10-second increments, whisking well between each cook time. If sauce becomes too thick or begins to clump, whisk in a dash of water.

7. Assemble each stacker by layering a Tater Tot waffle, 1 sausage patty, one-fourth of the spinach, 1 fried egg, and a drizzle of hollandaise sauce. Serve immediately.

PER SERVING

Calories: 548
Fat: 45g
Protein: 17g
Sodium: 1,160mg

Fiber: 3g
Carbohydrates: 15g
Sugar: 1g

LEMON POPPY SEED PANCAKES WITH MIXED BERRY COMPOTE

The insider secret to perfectly tender pancakes is to not overmix the batter. Remember, less is more when you have the whisk. Don't let a few lumps intimidate you. If you want to change up the types of fruit in the compote, go for it! Frozen blueberries, peaches, mangoes, blackberries, or cherries make delicious substitutions. Also, if you prefer a chunkier compote, keep the fruit whole instead of mashing it.

SERVES: 5
PREP TIME: 10 minutes
COOK TIME: 15 minutes
TOTAL TIME: 25 minutes

Compote

1 pound frozen unsweetened strawberries

1 pound frozen unsweetened raspberries

3 tablespoons lemon juice

1 cup granulated sugar

$\frac{2}{3}$ cup water

Pancakes

3 cups all-purpose flour

$\frac{1}{2}$ cup granulated sugar

2 tablespoons plus 1 teaspoon baking powder

1 teaspoon kosher salt

Zest of 2 medium lemons

3 tablespoons poppy seeds

6 tablespoons salted butter, melted

$2\frac{1}{3}$ cups whole milk

2 large eggs

Continued on next page

LEMON POPPY SEED PANCAKES WITH MIXED BERRY COMPOTE CONT.

1. To make the compote, in a medium saucepan, combine all compote ingredients and place over medium heat. Stir occasionally until fruit has softened, about 7 minutes. Use a potato masher or back of a wooden spoon to mash berries. Cook for another minute, then remove from heat.

2. While compote is cooking, make the pancakes. In a large bowl, whisk together flour, sugar, baking powder, salt, lemon zest, and poppy seeds.

3. In a separate medium bowl, whisk together melted butter, milk, and eggs until eggs are completely incorporated.

4. Preheat griddle to medium heat.

5. Create a well in center of the dry mixture, then add liquid mixture to it. Whisk until just combined; do not overmix. Batter will be slightly thick and lumpy. Allow batter to rest for 3 minutes.

6. Lightly spray griddle with nonstick spray and scoop ¼ cup batter per pancake onto hot surface (depending on the size of the griddle, you may need to work in batches to make approximately 20 pancakes). Cook until bubbles form in the center of the batter and edges are beginning to set, about 2 minutes. Flip and cook until lightly golden brown, about 2 minutes. Serve immediately with warm compote.

PER SERVING

Calories: 837
Fat: 20g
Protein: 16g
Sodium: 1,339mg

Fiber: 11g
Carbohydrates: 146g
Sugar: 75g

MONKEY BREAD MUFFINS

If you aren't aware of what monkey bread is, these muffins are about to become your new favorite! These decadent muffins are a perfect treat on a special morning, like a family birthday. You do need to thaw the biscuits, but you can do that in just a few minutes. They are best hot from the oven, but if by some miracle you have any left over, just toss them in the microwave for a few seconds to warm them up.

SERVES: 6
PREP TIME: 10 minutes
COOK TIME: 16 minutes
TOTAL TIME: 26 minutes

Ingredients

7 frozen raw biscuits

½ cup granulated sugar

1½ teaspoons cinnamon

4 tablespoons salted butter, melted

⅓ cup confectioners' sugar

2 tablespoons 1% milk

PER SERVING

Calories: 295	Fiber: 1g
Fat: 11g	Carbohydrates: 45g
Protein: 3g	Sugar: 24g
Sodium: 447mg	

1. Preheat oven to 375°F. Grease a 6-cup muffin tin with nonstick spray.

2. Lay biscuits flat on a microwave-safe plate and microwave at 30 percent power in 30-second increments until thawed, flipping biscuits over after each increment. Thawing will take 4–5 times total.

3. In a small bowl, combine granulated sugar and cinnamon.

4. Use scissors to cut each biscuit into eight even pieces. Dip each piece first in the butter, then toss in the cinnamon sugar to coat completely. Put nine pieces in each muffin cup and bake until golden brown and centers are set, 16–18 minutes.

5. While muffins bake, in a small bowl, combine confectioners' sugar and milk until smooth to form a glaze. Drizzle glaze over the baked muffins and serve immediately.

SWEET POTATO BREAKFAST SKILLET

This scrumptious and healthy breakfast option is chock-full of veggies and packed with flavor. It's loaded with sweet potatoes, mushrooms, spinach, onions, and peppers, then finished off with sunny-side-up eggs, which produce a heavenly gravy for all those vegetables. Feel free to add some grated cheese on top—a sharp Cheddar, pepper jack, or feta would be delicious.

SERVES: 4
PREP TIME: 5 minutes
COOK TIME: 10 minutes
TOTAL TIME: 15 minutes

Ingredients

2 tablespoons salted butter

1 cup frozen chopped onions

1 cup frozen sliced white mushrooms

¾ cup frozen chopped green bell peppers

1 teaspoon kosher salt, divided

½ teaspoon ground black pepper, divided

1 (10-ounce) bag frozen diced sweet potatoes

¾ cup frozen chopped spinach

4 large eggs

PER SERVING

Calories: 224
Fat: 10g
Protein: 10g
Sodium: 734mg

Fiber: 3g
Carbohydrates: 22g
Sugar: 3g

1. Heat a large skillet over high heat. When hot, add butter, onions, mushrooms, bell peppers, ¾ teaspoon salt, and ¼ teaspoon black pepper. Sauté until vegetables are softened and any moisture has evaporated, about 3–4 minutes. Add sweet potatoes and spinach. Cook until potatoes begin to soften, about 3–4 minutes.

2. Reduce heat to medium-high and create four wells inside the vegetables. Crack one egg into each and sprinkle remaining ¼ teaspoon each of salt and black pepper over all the eggs. Cover skillet with a lid and cook until eggs reach desired doneness, about 2–3 minutes for soft yolks and 4–5 minutes for firm. Serve immediately.

QUICK BREAKFAST PIZZA

Serving pizza for breakfast is how you send the kids to school ready to crush their day while also earning instant hero status in their eyes. Use your creativity with these pizzas and see what flavor combinations your family prefers. Mushrooms, bacon, ham, jalapeños, and olives would all be excellent substitutions for any of the ingredients listed. You could also make one large breakfast pizza by substituting the pita breads for a large precooked pizza dough sold in the bread aisle of your store.

SERVES: 4
PREP TIME: 10 minutes
COOK TIME: 12 minutes
TOTAL TIME: 22 minutes

Ingredients

1 tablespoon salted butter

¼ cup frozen chopped onions

¼ cup frozen chopped green bell peppers

⅓ cup frozen hash brown potatoes

½ teaspoon kosher salt, divided

¼ teaspoon ground black pepper, divided

6 large eggs, beaten

4 precooked frozen breakfast sausage links

2 (6") pita flatbreads

4 ounces cream cheese

1½ cups (6 ounces) shredded pepper jack cheese

1. Preheat oven to 400°F.

2. Heat a large nonstick skillet over high heat. When hot, add butter, onions, bell peppers, potatoes, ¼ teaspoon salt, and ⅛ teaspoon black pepper. Sauté until vegetables soften, about 3–4 minutes. Remove vegetables from skillet and set aside.

3. Return skillet to high heat and grease with nonstick spray. Add eggs, remaining ¼ teaspoon salt, and remaining ⅛ teaspoon black pepper. Stir and cook until eggs are firm, about 3–4 minutes, then remove from heat.

4. On a microwave-safe plate, thaw sausages in microwave on high for 1 minute, then slice.

5. To assemble, place pitas on rimmed baking sheet. Divide cream cheese evenly between them and spread onto surface. Then cover with eggs, vegetables, and pepper jack. Bake until cheese melts and edges of pitas toast, about 6–8 minutes. Serve immediately.

PER SERVING

Calories: 560
Fat: 38g
Protein: 28g
Sodium: 1,129mg

Fiber: 1g
Carbohydrates: 23g
Sugar: 3g

PANCAKE SAUSAGE DIPPERS WITH BUTTERMILK SYRUP

There will be sticky fingers as a result of this incredibly fun and tasty breakfast! If you are short on time, you can certainly serve these with your favorite store-bought maple syrup, but promise me you will come back and try the buttermilk syrup when you have time.

SERVES: 5
PREP TIME: 10 minutes
COOK TIME: 15 minutes
TOTAL TIME: 25 minutes

Pancake Sausage Dippers

10 precooked frozen breakfast
  sausage links

1½ cups all-purpose flour

½ cup granulated sugar

4 teaspoons baking powder

½ teaspoon kosher salt

1¼ cups whole milk

1 large egg

3 tablespoons salted butter, melted

Buttermilk Syrup

1½ cups granulated sugar

¾ cup 1% buttermilk

4 tablespoons salted butter

2 tablespoons light corn syrup

1 teaspoon baking soda

2 teaspoons vanilla extract

PER SERVING

Calories: 871
Fat: 34g
Protein: 15g
Sodium: 1,459mg

Fiber: 1g
Carbohydrates: 122g
Sugar: 92g

1. Preheat griddle to medium-high heat. Warm sausage in microwave on high for 1 minute, then cut each link in half lengthwise, creating 20 pieces of sausage. Set aside.

2. In a medium bowl, whisk together flour, sugar, baking powder, and salt. In a separate medium bowl, whisk together milk, egg, and butter until egg is completely incorporated. Create a well in the center of dry mixture, then add liquid mixture to it. Whisk until just combined; do not overmix. Batter will be slightly thick and lumpy. Allow batter to rest for 3 minutes.

3. Place sausages on the griddle and top each with 3 tablespoons pancake batter, making long, thin link-shaped pancakes. Cook until lightly golden brown, about 2 minutes, then flip to cook about 2 minutes on other side.

4. To make the syrup, in a large saucepan, combine sugar, buttermilk, butter, corn syrup, and baking soda (ingredients will expand, so be sure to use a large saucepan). Heat over medium-high heat, stirring frequently, until mixture comes to a full boil. Reduce heat and gently boil for 7 minutes, continuing to stir frequently. Remove from heat and add vanilla. Serve warm.

MIXED BERRY STREUSEL FRENCH TOAST BAKE

Take French toast to new heights with these individual bakes loaded with a smooth cinnamon custard, berries, and a dynamite streusel topping. The tartness of the berries perfectly balances the sweetness of the custard and topping. There's no need for any syrup on these babies! You can also make these the night before, cover them tightly with plastic wrap (store the streusel separately), store in the refrigerator overnight, then add streusel and bake them in the morning as directed.

SERVES: 6
PREP TIME: 10 minutes
COOK TIME: 20 minutes
TOTAL TIME: 30 minutes

Ingredients

3 large eggs

¾ cup 1% milk

3 tablespoons heavy cream

1½ tablespoons granulated sugar

6 tablespoons brown sugar, divided

1½ teaspoons vanilla extract

1 teaspoon cinnamon, divided

⅛ teaspoon ground nutmeg

6 slices potato bread, cut into ½" cubes

⅓ cup frozen raspberries

⅓ cup frozen blueberries

3 tablespoons all-purpose flour

2½ tablespoons salted butter

PER SERVING

Calories: 292
Fat: 10g
Protein: 9g
Sodium: 213mg

Fiber: 3g
Carbohydrates: 39g
Sugar: 23g

1. Preheat oven to 425°F. Grease six (7-ounce) ramekins with nonstick spray and place on a rimmed baking sheet.

2. In a large bowl, beat together eggs, milk, cream, granulated sugar, 3 tablespoons brown sugar, vanilla, ¾ teaspoon cinnamon, and nutmeg. Add cubed bread to bowl. Add raspberries and blueberries and mix well. Divide bread mixture evenly among ramekins.

3. In a medium bowl, combine flour, remaining 3 tablespoons brown sugar, and remaining ¼ teaspoon cinnamon. Using a pastry cutter or two forks, cut butter into dry ingredients until mixture is the size of small peas. Crumble over the top of the ramekins and bake about 20 minutes. Serve immediately.

BREAKFAST TATER TOT CASSEROLE

This is a robust egg bake filled with spinach, mushrooms, onions, cheese, and Tater Tots. It's vegetarian as written, but add some ham, sausage, or bacon if you prefer. Just be sure meats are fully cooked before adding them to the dish. If you are short on time in the morning, assemble the dish the night before, cover and refrigerate it, then bake it the next day.

SERVES: 6

PREP TIME: 7 minutes

COOK TIME: 23 minutes

TOTAL TIME: 30 minutes

Ingredients

1 tablespoon salted butter

½ cup frozen chopped onions

½ cup frozen sliced white mushrooms

½ cup frozen chopped spinach

¾ teaspoon kosher salt, divided

4 large eggs

1 cup 1% milk

¼ teaspoon ground black pepper

1 cup (4 ounces) shredded Cheddar cheese

1 pound frozen Tater Tots

PER SERVING

Calories: 282

Fat: 18g

Protein: 12g

Sodium: 882mg

Fiber: 2g

Carbohydrates: 16g

Sugar: 4g

1. Preheat oven to 425°F. Grease a 2-quart 7" × 11" baking pan with nonstick spray.

2. Heat a large skillet over high heat. When hot, add butter, onions, mushrooms, spinach, and ¼ teaspoon salt. Sauté until vegetables soften and any moisture has evaporated, about 3–4 minutes. Spread evenly in prepared baking pan.

3. In a small bowl, beat together eggs, milk, remaining ½ teaspoon salt, and pepper. Add to baking pan and top with Cheddar.

4. Heat Tater Tots in the microwave to thaw, about 2 minutes. Arrange on top of cheese layer and bake until eggs are set, 20–22 minutes. Serve hot.

BREAKFAST BURRITOS

These customizable burritos make a filling breakfast on the go for kids and adults alike. Filled with nutrients and protein, they'll keep you full all morning. You can also make a few batches of these, wrap them tightly, and freeze them. When you need them, just reheat in the microwave for 4–6 minutes, flipping over halfway through the cooking time.

SERVES: 6
PREP TIME: 5 minutes
COOK TIME: 15 minutes
TOTAL TIME: 20 minutes

Ingredients

2 tablespoons salted butter

1 cup frozen chopped onions

½ cup frozen chopped green bell peppers

2 cups frozen shredded hash brown potatoes

¾ teaspoon kosher salt, divided

¼ teaspoon ground black pepper, divided

8 precooked frozen breakfast sausage links

6 large eggs, beaten

6 (12") flour tortillas

1½ cups (6 ounces) shredded pepper jack cheese

2 medium Roma tomatoes, cored and diced

1. Heat a large nonstick skillet over high heat. When hot, add butter, onions, and bell peppers. Sauté until vegetables are softened and any moisture has evaporated, about 3–4 minutes. Add potatoes, ½ teaspoon salt, and ⅛ teaspoon pepper. Stir to combine, then let potatoes sit and brown on the bottom. Stir and let bottom brown one more time, about 8 minutes. Remove vegetables from skillet and set aside.

2. Microwave sausages on high just long enough to thaw, about 45 seconds. Chop into smaller pieces.

3. Return skillet to high heat and lightly grease with nonstick spray. Add eggs, sausage, remaining ¼ teaspoon salt, and remaining ⅛ teaspoon pepper. Stir and cook eggs to desired doneness, about 3–5 minutes. Remove from heat.

4. Heat tortillas in microwave on high for 30 seconds to soften them. Build each burrito with potato mixture, eggs, ¼ cup pepper jack, and tomatoes. Tuck in the ends before tightly rolling up. Serve.

PER SERVING

Calories: 748
Fat: 33g
Protein: 29g
Sodium: 1,660mg

Fiber: 5g
Carbohydrates: 77g
Sugar: 7g

BROWNED BUTTER BLUEBERRY STREUSEL MUFFINS

The browned butter in this muffin recipe creates an amazing depth of flavor. The streusel topping adds a nice crunch and sweetness. You can also make these gems with frozen raspberries instead of blueberries or a mixture of both berries. Try making a double batch and freezing some for later. Just wrap each muffin tightly with plastic wrap before freezing for up to 3 months.

SERVES: 9
PREP TIME: 8 minutes
COOK TIME: 22 minutes
TOTAL TIME: 30 minutes

Muffins

7 tablespoons salted butter

1½ cups all-purpose flour

¾ cup granulated sugar

1½ teaspoons baking powder

¾ teaspoon kosher salt

1 cup frozen blueberries

⅓ cup buttermilk

1 large egg

1 large egg yolk

1 teaspoon vanilla extract

Streusel Topping

½ cup all-purpose flour

3 tablespoons granulated sugar

3 tablespoons salted butter

PER SERVING

Calories: 323
Fat: 13g
Protein: 4g
Sodium: 395mg

Fiber: 1g
Carbohydrates: 45g
Sugar: 23g

1. Preheat oven to 400°F. Line a 9-cup muffin tin with paper liners.

2. To make the muffins, in a small saucepan over medium-high heat, melt butter. It will crackle and pop after it melts, then begin to turn a deep brown color and create some foam about 4–5 minutes later. Pour into a bowl to cool.

3. While butter browns, mix together flour, sugar, baking powder, salt, and blueberries in a large bowl. Set aside.

4. In a small bowl, whisk together buttermilk, egg, egg yolk, and vanilla. While whisking, drizzle in the browned butter. Make a well in the dry ingredients and pour liquid ingredients in it. Carefully fold the two together just until the batter barely comes together. Do not overmix. Divide among all muffin cups.

5. To make the streusel, in a small bowl, combine flour and sugar. Using a pastry cutter or two forks, cut butter into dry ingredients until mixture is the size of small peas. Sprinkle over each muffin and bake until the middle of the muffin springs back when touched, 18–20 minutes. Serve.

TROPICAL YOGURT PARFAITS

You'll sense some island vibes with this layered treat—pineapple, mandarin oranges, bananas, macadamia nuts, and coconut are complemented by vanilla Greek yogurt for a unique breakfast. The beauty of parfaits for breakfast, besides being lightning fast, is that they can be individualized for each member of your family. Someone doesn't like coconut? Just leave it out or try subbing in some granola instead.

SERVES: 4
PREP TIME: 5 minutes
COOK TIME: 5 minutes
TOTAL TIME: 10 minutes

Ingredients

2 cups frozen chopped pineapple

1 cup roughly chopped macadamia nuts

1 cup sweetened coconut flakes

4 cups nonfat vanilla Greek yogurt

2 medium bananas, peeled and chopped

1 (15-ounce) can mandarin oranges
   packed in juice, drained

1. In a medium microwave-safe bowl, microwave pineapple at 30 percent power in 30-second increments. Stir between each increment. Depending on your microwave's wattage, it will take about 4–5 times to thaw the pineapple. Chop thawed pineapple into bite-sized pieces.

2. Heat a medium skillet over medium-high heat. When hot, add nuts and coconut. Stir and allow nuts and coconut to lightly toast, about 3–4 minutes. Remove from skillet to cool.

3. Divide the following ingredients among four individual bowls or parfait dishes, layering in this order: yogurt, nuts and coconut, pineapple, bananas, oranges, more yogurt, and a few more nuts and coconut. Serve.

PER SERVING

Calories: 649
Fat: 31g
Protein: 25g
Sodium: 150mg

Fiber: 9g
Carbohydrates: 74g
Sugar: 57g

EGG, SAUSAGE, AND CHEESE ENGLISH MUFFIN SANDWICHES

Skip that drive-through on your way to work and make these at home instead. Not only do they taste better and use higher-quality ingredients, but making them at home will save you money as well. You can make enough for the whole week, wrap them individually, and store them in the refrigerator. Then before you leave for work, toss them in the microwave for about a minute until they are hot.

SERVES: 8
PREP TIME: 5 minutes
COOK TIME: 15 minutes
TOTAL TIME: 20 minutes

Ingredients

6 large eggs

¼ cup 1% milk

½ teaspoon kosher salt

¼ teaspoon ground black pepper

8 English muffins, split

8 precooked frozen sausage patties

8 slices American cheese

PER SERVING

Calories: 446
Fat: 27g
Protein: 21g
Sodium: 1,056mg
Fiber: 2g
Carbohydrates: 28g
Sugar: 4g

1. Preheat oven to 350°F. Grease a 7" × 11" baking dish with nonstick spray.

2. In a medium bowl, whisk together eggs, milk, salt, and pepper. Pour into prepared baking dish and bake until eggs don't jiggle when you shake the dish, 15–17 minutes. Set aside.

3. While the eggs are baking, toast English muffins and heat sausage in the microwave according to package directions.

4. Cut eggs into eight pieces and assemble each sandwich on an English muffin with an egg patty, sausage patty, and slice of American cheese. Serve.

Chapter Three
SIDE DISHES

THIS CHAPTER FEATURES CLASSICS LIKE SALADS, POTA-
TOES, AND VEGETABLES, BUT IT ALSO INCLUDES A FEW
SURPRISES TO KEEP YOUR MENU PLANNING INTEREST-
ING. MOST OF THESE DISHES CAN BE EASILY PAIRED WITH
YOUR FAVORITE CUTS OF BEEF, CHICKEN, PORK, OR FISH,
NO MATTER IF YOU ARE GRILLING, ROASTING, OR BROIL-
ING THEM. A GREAT NEW SIDE DISH IS ALSO AN INNO-
VATIVE WAY TO RESCUE ANY DINNER THAT INCLUDES
PULLING LEFTOVERS FROM THE FRIDGE. AS A MATTER
OF FACT, SOME OF THESE SELECTIONS ARE SUBSTANTIAL
ENOUGH TO SERVE COMPLETELY ON THEIR OWN AS A
MAIN DISH. YOU COULD EVEN PAIR TWO OR THREE OF
THEM TOGETHER FOR A SIDE DISH SMORGASBORD.

ROASTED PARMESAN CREAMED PEARL ONIONS

Pearl onions are simply baby onions. Because they are young, pearl onions don't have the sharpness of flavor found in full-grown onions. Instead, they have a natural sweetness that pairs well with the saltiness of the fresh Parmesan cheese. Anytime you are cooking steaks on the grill, toss these in the oven because they are heavenly together. If red meat isn't your thing, serve them alongside grilled chicken, pork, or seafood.

SERVES: 4
PREP TIME: 5 minutes
COOK TIME: 21 minutes
TOTAL TIME: 26 minutes

Ingredients

1 teaspoon extra-virgin olive oil

1 (12-ounce) bag frozen pearl onions

¼ teaspoon kosher salt, divided

¼ teaspoon ground black pepper, divided

1 teaspoon salted butter

1 cube frozen crushed garlic

⅔ cup heavy cream

2 tablespoons water

1 teaspoon red wine vinegar

⅓ cup (or about 1 ounce) freshly grated Parmesan cheese

PER SERVING

Calories: 231
Fat: 18g
Protein: 3g
Sodium: 337mg

Fiber: 1g
Carbohydrates: 10g
Sugar: 5g

1. Preheat oven to 450°F. Lightly grease an 11" × 7" baking pan with nonstick spray.

2. Heat a large skillet over high heat. When hot, add oil, onions, ⅛ teaspoon salt, and ⅛ teaspoon pepper. Sauté onions until they begin to brown, about 4–5 minutes. Transfer onions to the prepared baking pan.

3. Return skillet to medium-high heat and add butter and garlic. Sauté for 1 minute. Add cream, water, and vinegar. Stir and allow mixture to come to a gentle boil, in about 3 minutes, before reducing heat. Simmer for 2–3 minutes to thicken the sauce.

4. Add remaining ⅛ teaspoon salt and ⅛ teaspoon pepper, then pour sauce over onions. Sprinkle Parmesan over the top and bake until bubbly and top is beginning to brown, about 12 minutes. If you want to continue to brown the top, you can place it under a broiler for an additional minute before serving.

PRALINE SWEET POTATOES

If you need an extra-special side dish for a holiday dinner, these individual ramekins of sweet potatoes are delectable! This recipe will convert anyone into a sweet potato lover. The instructions call for 7-ounce ramekins, but feel free to use any size that you have on hand. If they are smaller, just shorten the bake time, and if they are larger, add a few more minutes.

SERVES: 6
PREP TIME: 12 minutes
COOK TIME: 18 minutes
TOTAL TIME: 30 minutes

Ingredients

2 (10-ounce) bags frozen diced
    sweet potatoes

¼ cup granulated sugar

1 large egg

6 tablespoons heavy cream

2 teaspoons vanilla extract

1½ tablespoons all purpose flour

½ cup brown sugar

3 tablespoons salted butter

½ cup chopped pecans

PER SERVING

Calories: 382
Fat: 17g
Protein: 3g
Sodium: 61mg

Fiber: 3g
Carbohydrates: 54g
Sugar: 27g

1. Preheat oven to 400°F. Place six (7-ounce) ramekins on a rimmed baking sheet and grease with nonstick spray.

2. Microwave sweet potatoes according to package directions, then place in a large bowl. Mash with a potato masher and add sugar, egg, cream, and vanilla. Mix well.

3. Divide sweet potato mixture among the prepared ramekins.

4. In a medium bowl, mix together flour and brown sugar. Using a pastry cutter or two forks, cut butter into dry ingredients until mixture is the size of small peas. Add the pecans and toss to combine. Sprinkle topping over the ramekins and bake until bubbly and topping begins to brown, about 18 minutes. Serve immediately.

VEGETABLE FRIED RICE

Ready to make takeout-quality fried rice at home? This fabulous recipe is loaded with tons of veggies and an authentic sauce. Be sure not to skip the freezer step—freezing the rice will keep it from becoming mushy when frying. (The cold grains reabsorb the starch released when initially cooked.) This recipe can easily be served as a main dish by adding chicken, pork, or shrimp.

SERVES: 6
PREP TIME: 10 minutes
COOK TIME: 12 minutes
TOTAL TIME: 22 minutes

Ingredients

1 (18-ounce) box frozen sticky white rice

2½ tablespoons soy sauce

1½ teaspoons oyster sauce

¾ teaspoon sesame oil

3½ tablespoons salted butter, divided

2 large eggs, beaten

1 cup frozen chopped onions

2 cubes frozen crushed garlic

4 medium white mushrooms, chopped

¼ teaspoon kosher salt

⅛ teaspoon ground black pepper

¾ cup frozen peas and carrots blend

2 medium green onions,
   trimmed and chopped

1. Follow directions on the box of rice to heat in the microwave. Spread hot rice onto a large plate, then place in the freezer to cool off for 10–15 minutes.

2. In a small bowl, combine soy sauce, oyster sauce, and oil. Set aside.

3. In a large nonstick skillet, heat 1 tablespoon butter on high heat, then cook eggs until firmly scrambled, about 2–3 minutes. Remove from skillet and set aside.

4. Return skillet to stove and add 1 tablespoon butter, onions, garlic, mushrooms, salt, and pepper. Sauté on high until mushrooms are cooked through, about 3–4 minutes.

5. Add remaining 1½ tablespoons butter to the skillet, along with the cold rice, cooked eggs, frozen peas and carrots, and onions. Stir well and fry rice in the butter for 2–3 minutes before adding soy sauce mixture and combining. Sprinkle with green onions and serve immediately.

PER SERVING

Calories: 243

Fat: 8g

Protein: 6g

Sodium: 607mg

Fiber: 1g

Carbohydrates: 33g

Sugar: 1g

PARMESAN GARLIC–ROASTED BRUSSELS SPROUTS

Yes, you really can roast frozen vegetables and end up with an impressive caramelized exterior! The key is to use a really hot oven temperature so that any moisture evaporates quickly, giving the sugars in the Brussels sprouts a chance to work their magic. If you love this simple vegetable recipe, try swapping in frozen cauliflower or broccoli for easy variations.

SERVES: 6
PREP TIME: 10 minutes
COOK TIME: 20 minutes
TOTAL TIME: 30 minutes

Ingredients

2 cubes frozen crushed garlic

3 tablespoons vegetable oil

1 teaspoon kosher salt

½ teaspoon ground black pepper

2 (12-ounce) bags frozen Brussels sprouts

⅓ cup freshly grated Parmesan cheese

PER SERVING

Calories: 135
Fat: 8g
Protein: 6g
Sodium: 507mg

Fiber: 4g
Carbohydrates: 10g
Sugar: 0g

1. Preheat oven to 450°F. Grease a rimmed baking sheet with nonstick spray.

2. In a medium bowl, mash garlic, oil, salt, and pepper together. Add Brussels sprouts and toss to coat. Spread in a single layer on baking sheet and roast for 8 minutes. (Hang on to the bowl.)

3. Remove sprouts from oven, cut each in half with a sharp knife, and toss once again in the bowl to coat cut side with the remaining oil and seasonings in the bowl. Return to pan and roast for another 12 minutes, flipping after 6 minutes. Top with Parmesan and serve immediately.

BUTTERNUT SQUASH GRATIN

This gratin will convince everyone in your family that they love butternut squash! The garlic butter mellows the sweetness of the squash, and who doesn't love a crunchy, cheesy topping on their veggies? If you are serving a bigger crowd and need to double this recipe, use a 2-quart pan and add an extra 10 minutes to the baking time.

SERVES: 4
PREP TIME: 5 minutes
COOK TIME: 22 minutes
TOTAL TIME: 27 minutes

Ingredients

1 (10-ounce) bag frozen butternut squash

3 tablespoons salted butter, melted

2 cubes frozen crushed garlic

¾ teaspoon kosher salt

¼ teaspoon ground black pepper

¼ cup panko bread crumbs

⅓ cup freshly grated Parmesan cheese

½ teaspoon dried parsley

1. Preheat oven to 425°F. Grease a 1-quart baking dish with nonstick spray.

2. Spread squash evenly in prepared baking dish.

3. In a small bowl, combine butter and garlic. Drizzle 2 tablespoons of the butter mixture over squash. Sprinkle salt and pepper on top.

4. Add bread crumbs, Parmesan, and parsley to remaining butter mixture, then spread over squash. Bake until hot and bubbly, 22–25 minutes. Serve immediately.

PER SERVING

Calories: 181
Fat: 10g
Protein: 4g
Sodium: 682mg

Fiber: 1g
Carbohydrates: 17g
Sugar: 2g

INDIVIDUAL CHEESY POTATO CASSEROLES

Bubbling with a divine cheese sauce and topped off with Parmesan panko crunchiness, these individual casseroles look as good as they taste. If you happen to have any leftovers, wrap the ramekins in plastic wrap, refrigerate for up to 5 days, and reheat them in the microwave whenever the craving hits.

SERVES: 8
PREP TIME: 10 minutes
COOK TIME: 20 minutes
TOTAL TIME: 30 minutes

Ingredients

1 (26-ounce) bag frozen shredded hash brown potatoes

5 tablespoons salted butter, melted, divided

1 (10-ounce) can cream of chicken soup

1 cup sour cream

1 cup 1% milk

2 medium green onions, trimmed and finely chopped

1½ cups (6 ounces) shredded sharp Cheddar cheese

¾ teaspoon kosher salt

½ teaspoon ground black pepper

¾ teaspoon garlic powder

¾ cup panko bread crumbs

2 tablespoons freshly grated Parmesan cheese

1. Preheat oven to 400°F. Spray eight (7-ounce) ramekins with nonstick spray and place on a baking sheet.

2. In the microwave on high, heat bag of potatoes to thaw, about 2 minutes. Divide thawed potatoes among the prepared ramekins. Drizzle 3 tablespoons butter over potatoes.

3. In a medium bowl, combine soup, sour cream, milk, onions, Cheddar, salt, pepper, and garlic powder. Spoon mixture evenly over ramekins.

4. In a small bowl, combine panko crumbs, Parmesan, and remaining 2 tablespoons butter. Top each ramekin with crumb mixture and bake until hot and bubbly, about 20 minutes. Serve immediately.

PER SERVING

Calories: 374
Fat: 22g
Protein: 11g
Sodium: 723mg

Fiber: 3g
Carbohydrates: 29g
Sugar: 3g

BAKED CAULIFLOWER TOTS

Your family will be asking for these every night for dinner, and you will happily oblige—not only are they fairly healthy, they are also supereasy to make. Florets of tasty and nutritious cauliflower get coated in Parmesan cheese and panko bread crumbs before being baked golden brown and perfectly crispy. You could also substitute frozen broccoli florets for the cauliflower if that's what you have on hand.

SERVES: 4
PREP TIME: 10 minutes
COOK TIME: 10 minutes
TOTAL TIME: 20 minutes

Ingredients

1 (12-ounce) bag frozen cauliflower florets

2 large eggs

1 tablespoon 1% milk

1 cup panko bread crumbs

⅓ cup freshly grated Parmesan cheese

½ teaspoon garlic powder

½ teaspoon Italian seasoning

¾ teaspoon kosher salt, divided

¼ teaspoon ground black pepper

PER SERVING

Calories: 106	Fiber: 2g
Fat: 3g	Carbohydrates: 15g
Protein: 6g	Sugar: 3g
Sodium: 359mg	

1. Preheat oven to 450°F. Grease a baking sheet with non-stick spray.

2. Microwave bag of cauliflower on high for 2 minutes, just long enough to slightly thaw the florets. Set aside.

3. In a small bowl, beat together eggs and milk until combined. Set aside.

4. In a small bowl, mix together bread crumbs, Parmesan, garlic powder, Italian seasoning, ½ teaspoon salt, and pepper.

5. Coat 3–4 pieces cauliflower at a time with egg mixture, then put into the bread-crumb mixture. Press the crumbs firmly into the cauliflower, then place on baking sheet. Continue until all cauliflower is coated. Bake until golden brown, about 10 minutes. Sprinkle finished tots with remaining ¼ teaspoon salt and serve.

LOADED ROASTED POTATO SALAD

If you love loaded baked potatoes with bacon, cheese, sour cream, and green onions, you will adore this warm potato salad. Most potato salads have too much mayonnaise, which overpowers the dressing, but this recipe has just a hint of it. It's delicious warm or cold. This recipe uses frozen potatoes O'Brien, which are frozen diced potatoes that also include chopped onions and bell peppers in the bag. You can find them with the other frozen potato products.

SERVES: 6
PREP TIME: 10 minutes
COOK TIME: 20 minutes
TOTAL TIME: 30 minutes

Ingredients

1 (28-ounce) bag frozen potatoes O'Brien

2 tablespoons vegetable oil

1¼ teaspoons kosher salt, divided

12 strips bacon

3 medium green onions, trimmed and chopped

¾ cup (3 ounces) shredded Cheddar cheese

¾ cup sour cream

6 tablespoons mayonnaise

1½ teaspoons ground black pepper

PER SERVING

Calories: 459
Fat: 32g
Protein: 15g
Sodium: 1,108mg

Fiber: 3g
Carbohydrates: 26g
Sugar: 1g

1. Preheat oven to 450°F. Grease a rimmed baking sheet with nonstick spray.

2. In a large bowl, toss together potatoes, oil, and ½ teaspoon salt. Spread onto baking sheet and bake until edges of potatoes are beginning to brown, about 18 minutes. Reserve empty bowl.

3. Heat a large skillet over high heat and cook bacon until crispy, about 5 minutes. Drain on paper towels and crumble into smaller pieces. Set aside.

4. In the large reserved bowl, mix together onions, Cheddar, sour cream, mayonnaise, pepper, remaining ¾ teaspoon salt, bacon, and cooked potatoes. Serve.

JICAMA AVOCADO CORN SALAD

This refreshing salad is perfect on a hot night beside your favorite grilled protein. The level of heat is completely in your control. If you like spicy food, finely dice the whole jalapeño, including the seeds and interior membrane. If not, just use the flesh for a hint of heat that fully complements the sweetness of the corn and jicama. You might also love this dish as a type of salsa, eaten straight with chips or on top of tacos.

SERVES: 8
PREP TIME: 10 minutes
COOK TIME: N/A
TOTAL TIME: 10 minutes

Ingredients

1 (10-ounce) bag frozen corn

2 medium avocados, peeled, pitted, and diced

3 medium Roma tomatoes, cored and diced

½ medium red onion, peeled and diced

½ cup diced jicama

½ bunch fresh cilantro, chopped

1 medium jalapeño pepper, seeded, cored, and minced

2 cubes frozen crushed garlic

Juice of 2 medium limes

2 tablespoons extra-virgin olive oil

1½ teaspoons kosher salt

½ teaspoon ground black pepper

PER SERVING

Calories: 150	Fiber: 4g
Fat: 8g	Carbohydrates: 18g
Protein: 3g	Sugar: 3g
Sodium: 448mg	

1. Place corn in a mesh strainer and run under cold water. Stir it around until it thaws, about 2 minutes. Place in a large bowl and add avocados, tomatoes, onion, jicama, cilantro, and jalapeño.

2. In a small bowl, whisk together garlic, lime juice, oil, salt, and black pepper. Add to the salad and mix well. Serve immediately.

CREAMY ONION RING AND GREEN BEAN BAKE

A creamy mushroom and onion sauce surrounds green beans topped with crispy onion rings in this casserole, which will put your mom's old recipe to shame. If you really like onion rings, use a bag and a half to take the onion ring game up a few notches.

SERVES: 6
PREP TIME: 5 minutes
COOK TIME: 25 minutes
TOTAL TIME: 30 minutes

Ingredients

1 (14-ounce) bag frozen onion rings

1 (16-ounce) bag frozen green beans

2 tablespoons salted butter

⅔ cup frozen chopped onions

3 cubes frozen crushed garlic

1 (10-ounce) bag frozen sliced white mushrooms

1¼ teaspoons kosher salt

½ teaspoon ground black pepper

3 tablespoons all-purpose flour

1½ cups 1% milk

½ cup heavy cream

1 tablespoon red wine vinegar

¼ cup freshly grated Parmesan cheese

1. Preheat oven to 400°F. Grease a 9" × 13" baking dish with nonstick spray.

2. Place onion rings on a rimmed baking sheet and bake for 8 minutes.

3. Cook green beans in microwave according to package directions. Set aside.

4. Heat a large skillet over high heat. When hot, add butter, onions, garlic, mushrooms, salt, and pepper. Cook until vegetables are softened and much of excess moisture evaporates, about 3–4 minutes.

5. Stir in flour and cook for 1 minute before adding milk and cream. Stir and allow sauce to thicken, about 2 minutes. Add vinegar, Parmesan, and green beans. Mix well and place in prepared baking dish. Top with baked onion rings and bake until hot and bubbly, 13–15 minutes. Serve warm.

PER SERVING

Calories: 308
Fat: 21g
Protein: 9g
Sodium: 809mg

Fiber: 4g
Carbohydrates: 36g
Sugar: 7g

SWEET PEA AND BACON SALAD

This is a classic summertime salad that pairs wonderfully with grilled burgers—or bring it to your next potluck. Sweet peas, thick-cut bacon, cheese, and onions are tossed in a creamy dressing. If you are short on time, instead of cooking the bacon at home, you can grab a bag of precooked real bacon bits as a substitute.

SERVES: 6
PREP TIME: 10 minutes
COOK TIME: 5 minutes
TOTAL TIME: 15 minutes

Ingredients

1 (16-ounce) bag frozen peas

½ cup frozen chopped onions

8 pieces thick-cut bacon

¾ cup (3 ounces) shredded Cheddar cheese

¼ cup mayonnaise

¼ cup sour cream

1 tablespoon red wine vinegar

1 tablespoon granulated sugar

½ teaspoon kosher salt

½ teaspoon ground black pepper

¼ teaspoon paprika

1. Place peas and onions in a mesh strainer and run under cool water until thawed, about 2 minutes. Place in a medium bowl.

2. Heat a large skillet over medium-high heat. When hot, add bacon and cook until crisp, about 5 minutes. Drain on paper towels. Crumble into smaller pieces and add to peas. Add Cheddar, mayonnaise, sour cream, vinegar, sugar, salt, pepper, and paprika to the bowl. Mix well to combine and serve.

PER SERVING

Calories: 316	Fiber: 4g
Fat: 20g	Carbohydrates: 14g
Protein: 16g	Sugar: 7g
Sodium: 817mg	

AVOCADO FETA BLT SALAD

There is no better way to eat tomatoes fresh from the garden than in this BLT salad, which is a healthier spin on the classic sandwich. You will love how the creamy avocado acts almost like a second dressing when you toss this gorgeous salad together. You could easily double this recipe and turn it into a main dish by adding some grilled chicken.

SERVES: 4
PREP TIME: 15 minutes
COOK TIME: 5 minutes
TOTAL TIME: 20 minutes

Ingredients

½ pound thick-cut bacon, chopped

¾ cup frozen corn

2 medium romaine lettuce hearts, chopped

2 medium Roma tomatoes, cored and diced

1 medium avocado, peeled, pitted, and diced

4 medium green onions, trimmed and chopped

1 cup (4 ounces) crumbled feta cheese

1 cube frozen crushed garlic

Juice of 1 medium lime

1½ tablespoons extra-virgin olive oil

½ teaspoon kosher salt

¼ teaspoon ground black pepper

1. Heat a large skillet over medium-high heat and cook bacon until brown and crispy, about 5 minutes. Drain on paper towels and set aside.

2. Place frozen corn in a mesh strainer and run under cold water for 1 minute until it thaws. Set aside.

3. In a large bowl, add romaine, tomatoes, avocado, corn, onions, feta, and bacon.

4. In a small bowl, whisk together garlic, lime juice, oil, salt, and pepper. Drizzle over the salad and toss together before serving.

PER SERVING

Calories: 395
Fat: 26g
Protein: 19g
Sodium: 1,054mg

Fiber: 10g
Carbohydrates: 23g
Sugar: 7g

BROCCOLI ALMOND STIR-FRY

This variation on a typical stir-fry provides an authentic Asian flavor to the broccoli, while the toasted almonds bring a delicious crunch to every bite. The heat on this is extremely subtle, so increase the amount of red pepper flakes if you like.

SERVES: 4
PREP TIME: 5 minutes
COOK TIME: 7 minutes
TOTAL TIME: 12 minutes

Ingredients

4 teaspoons soy sauce

1 teaspoon oyster sauce

½ teaspoon sesame oil

¾ teaspoon granulated sugar

⅛ teaspoon red pepper flakes

¼ teaspoon cornstarch

1 teaspoon vegetable oil

1 (12-ounce) bag frozen broccoli florets

1 cube frozen crushed ginger

1 cube frozen crushed garlic

2 tablespoons toasted slivered almonds

1. In a small bowl, combine soy and oyster sauces, sesame oil, sugar, red pepper flakes, and cornstarch. Set aside.

2. Heat a large skillet over high heat. When hot, add vegetable oil, broccoli, ginger, and garlic. Sauté for 3 minutes, then add half the soy sauce mixture. Continue to cook for another 2 minutes, then add remaining sauce. Cook until broccoli is still firm, about 2 more minutes. Top with almonds and serve.

PER SERVING

Calories: 69
Fat: 3g
Protein: 4g
Sodium: 364mg

Fiber: 0g
Carbohydrates: 7g
Sugar: 1g

MINI CORN SOUFFLÉS

Some people call these corn puddings or spoonbread—but whatever you call them, these are terrific! Each bite is tender and sweet thanks to using corn in two different ways. You will also love how this dish comes together in a matter of minutes and that there's no need to thaw the frozen corn before mixing it into the soufflé. If you wanted to make one big soufflé instead of muffin-sized individual servings, you could bake this in a 7" × 11" pan at 350°F for 50–55 minutes.

SERVES: 12
PREP TIME: 5 minutes
COOK TIME: 17 minutes
TOTAL TIME: 22 minutes

Ingredients

4 tablespoons salted butter, melted

1 cup sour cream

2 large eggs

1 (15-ounce) can creamed corn

1¾ cups frozen corn

1 (8.5-ounce) box Jiffy corn muffin mix

PER SERVING

Calories: 208
Fat: 10g
Protein: 4g
Sodium: 319mg

Fiber: 1g
Carbohydrates: 26g
Sugar: 6g

1. Preheat oven to 425°F. Grease a 12-cup muffin tin with nonstick spray.

2. In a medium bowl, mix together butter, sour cream, eggs, and creamed corn. Add frozen corn and muffin mix. Mix just until combined.

3. Divide among muffin cups and bake until set in the middle, 17–19 minutes. Serve.

Chapter Four

CHICKEN MAIN DISHES

CHICKEN IS AMERICA'S FAVORITE MEAL FOUNDATION BECAUSE IT IS QUICK TO PREPARE, GREAT-TASTING, PACKED WITH HEALTHY PROTEIN, EASY ON THE BUDGET, AND VERY VERSATILE, COMPLEMENTING ALL TYPES OF CUISINES. IN FACT, THE AVERAGE AMERICAN CONSUMES A SURPRISING 93 POUNDS OF CHICKEN EVERY YEAR, SO WE ALL NEED PLENTY OF IDEAS.

IF YOU HAVEN'T ALREADY DISCOVERED THE PRE-COOKED FROZEN CHICKEN SELECTIONS AT YOUR GROCERY STORE, THEY WILL SIGNIFICANTLY REDUCE THE TIME YOU NEED TO GET DINNER ON THE TABLE. YOUR GROCER'S FREEZER IS A TREASURE TROVE OF PERFECTLY SEASONED AND COOKED BONELESS, SKINLESS CHICKEN BREAST MEAT. YOU CAN FIND IT IN MULTIPLE FORMS AS WELL—DICED, SHREDDED, OR GRILLED AND CUT INTO STRIPS. THE RECIPES IN THIS CHAPTER FEATURE SOME FAMILIAR FAVORITES ALONGSIDE SOME MORE UNIQUE AND INTERESTING COMBINATIONS.

BAKED BARBECUE CHICKEN SLIDERS

These little gems will be on high demand in your menu rotation, especially with those sweet Hawaiian rolls slathered in Parmesan garlic butter. If your store doesn't carry the pulled chicken breasts, just grab a bag of diced chicken instead and chop the pieces up even smaller before following the recipe.

SERVES: 12
PREP TIME: 10 minutes
COOK TIME: 13 minutes
TOTAL TIME: 23 minutes

Ingredients

1 (20-ounce) bag frozen fully cooked pulled chicken breast

¾ cup barbecue sauce

1 teaspoon Worcestershire sauce

½ teaspoon smoked paprika

12 sweet Hawaiian slider rolls

1 cup (4 ounces) shredded mozzarella cheese

1 cup (4 ounces) shredded Cheddar cheese

3 tablespoons salted butter, melted

¾ teaspoon garlic powder

¾ teaspoon dried parsley

1½ tablespoons freshly grated Parmesan cheese

PER SERVING

Calories: 283
Fat: 12g
Protein: 19g
Sodium: 789mg

Fiber: 0g
Carbohydrates: 25g
Sugar: 11g

1. Preheat oven to 350°F.

2. Place chicken in a medium microwave-safe bowl and microwave on high in 45-second increments, just until chicken softens. Add barbecue sauce, Worcestershire, and paprika. Mix together to evenly coat chicken.

3. Remove tops of slider rolls. Place bottom part of rolls in a 9" × 13" baking pan. Divide chicken evenly among rolls and top with mozzarella and Cheddar. Replace slider tops.

4. In a small bowl, mix together butter, garlic powder, and parsley. Spread over bun tops, then sprinkle with Parmesan. Bake uncovered until cheese melts, approximately 13–15 minutes. Serve immediately.

SOUTHWEST CHICKEN QUESADILLAS

Is time supershort for dinner tonight? These yummy quesadillas are your salvation. Serve them hot from the griddle and get creative with toppings—sour cream or guacamole are delicious slathered on top. If you like a little more spice, feel free to substitute pepper jack cheese for the Cheddar.

SERVES: 15
PREP TIME: 10 minutes
COOK TIME: 10 minutes
TOTAL TIME: 20 minutes

Ingredients

1½ cups frozen fully cooked diced chicken breast

1½ cups frozen corn

1 (15-ounce) can black beans, drained and rinsed

1 (7-ounce) can diced green chilies, undrained

Juice of 1 medium lime

¾ teaspoon kosher salt

½ teaspoon ground black pepper

¾ teaspoon garlic powder

½ teaspoon onion powder

15 (6") flour tortillas

2 cups (8 ounces) shredded Cheddar cheese

1. Preheat griddle to medium-high heat.

2. In a medium microwave-safe bowl, heat chicken in 45-second increments until it thaws. Chop up any bigger pieces of chicken, then add corn, beans, green chilies, lime juice, salt, pepper, garlic powder, and onion powder. Mix well.

3. To assemble each quesadilla, sprinkle approximately 1 tablespoon Cheddar on half a tortilla, scoop on 2 tablespoons filling, then add more Cheddar on top. Fold over the top of the tortilla and cook on the griddle until first side browns, about 2 minutes. Flip over and cook until second side browns and cheese melts, about 2 minutes. Serve immediately.

PER SERVING

Calories: 213
Fat: 7g
Protein: 12g
Sodium: 880mg

Fiber: 3g
Carbohydrates: 25g
Sugar: 2g

SOUTHWEST CHICKEN TORTILLA SOUP

If you're craving a hearty, healthy, and delectable dinner on a cold night, this soup fits the bill. The use of mild green chilies provides the ideal hint of heat. Add chopped avocado, fresh cilantro, sour cream, and a squeeze of lime juice to highlight the classic Southwestern flavors.

SERVES: 6
PREP TIME: 15 minutes
COOK TIME: 10 minutes
TOTAL TIME: 25 minutes

Ingredients

1 tablespoon canola oil

1½ cups frozen chopped onions

3 cubes frozen crushed garlic

2 teaspoons chili powder

2 teaspoons dried oregano

1 (7-ounce) can diced green chilies, undrained

1 (15-ounce) can petite diced tomatoes, undrained

1 (32-ounce) box chicken broth

2 (15-ounce) cans black beans, drained and rinsed

1½ cups frozen corn

1 (22-ounce) bag frozen fully cooked diced chicken breast

1 cup (4 ounces) shredded Cheddar cheese

1 (12-ounce) bag corn tortilla chips

PER SERVING

Calories: 726	Fiber: 16g
Fat: 23g	Carbohydrates: 83g
Protein: 43g	Sugar: 10g
Sodium: 2,163mg	

1. Heat a large pot over high heat. When hot, add oil, onions, and garlic. Sauté for 2–3 minutes until onions are softened, then add chili powder and oregano. Stir and cook for another minute.

2. Add green chilies and tomatoes (without draining), followed by broth, beans, corn, and chicken breast. Bring to a boil, then reduce heat to low and simmer for 5 minutes.

3. Serve in bowls topped with Cheddar and crumbled tortilla chips.

POPCORN CHICKEN BLT PASTA SALAD

This fun take on a pasta salad is a decadent treat! Warm, crunchy bites of popcorn chicken are studded throughout this creamy pasta salad among the hits of bacon, lettuce, and tomato. Your kids will even love bringing leftovers to school with them the next day, but honestly, there aren't usually many leftovers with this recipe, so you might want to make a double batch.

SERVES: 6
PREP TIME: 10 minutes
COOK TIME: 16 minutes
TOTAL TIME: 26 minutes

Salad

1 (24-ounce) bag frozen popcorn chicken

¾ teaspoon kosher salt

8 ounces uncooked bowtie pasta

½ pound thick-cut bacon, chopped

1 large romaine lettuce heart, cored and chopped

3 medium Roma tomatoes, cored and chopped

½ small red onion, thinly sliced

1 cup (4 ounces) shredded sharp Cheddar cheese

Dressing

¾ cup mayonnaise

3 tablespoons red wine vinegar

2 tablespoons granulated sugar

1½ teaspoons kosher salt

¾ teaspoon ground black pepper

1. To make the salad, bake chicken according to package directions. Set aside.

2. In a medium pot, bring 2 quarts water to a boil. Add salt and pasta. Cook for 11 minutes, drain, and lightly rinse with cold water.

3. In a medium skillet on high heat, cook bacon about 5 minutes until crisp. Drain on paper towels.

4. In a large bowl, place lettuce, tomatoes, onion, Cheddar, bacon, pasta, and chicken.

5. To make the dressing, in a small bowl, mix together all dressing ingredients.

6. Add dressing to large bowl and toss with salad before serving.

PER SERVING

Calories: 802

Fat: 41g

Protein: 30g

Sodium: 1,068mg

Fiber: 5g

Carbohydrates: 74g

Sugar: 9g

BUFFALO CHICKEN FLATBREADS

These quick and scrumptious flatbreads are perfect for a busy weeknight meal or to serve at your next big-game feast. If you aren't a fan of blue cheese, you can easily substitute feta cheese or just leave it off completely. On the other hand, if you love blue cheese, try swapping out the ranch for blue cheese dressing to add even more of that flavor.

SERVES: 4
PREP TIME: 10 minutes
COOK TIME: 12 minutes
TOTAL TIME: 22 minutes

Ingredients

2 ounces cream cheese, softened

¼ cup ranch dressing

¼ cup buffalo wing sauce

4 (8") naan flatbreads

1 cup (4 ounces) shredded
   mozzarella cheese

1 cup (4 ounces) shredded
   Cheddar cheese

¼ cup blue cheese crumbles

2 cups frozen fully cooked diced
   chicken breast

1 medium green onion, trimmed
   and chopped

PER SERVING

Calories: 654
Fat: 28g
Protein: 43g
Sodium: 1,965mg

Fiber: 2g
Carbohydrates: 50g
Sugar: 6g

1. Preheat oven to 425°F.

2. In a small bowl, mix together cream cheese, ranch, and wing sauce.

3. Place flatbreads on two ungreased sheet pans and spread cream cheese mixture onto each. Top each with mozzarella, Cheddar, and blue cheeses, followed by the frozen chicken and onion. Bake until cheese is hot and bubbly, about 12 minutes. Serve immediately.

CRUNCHY PARMESAN CHICKEN WRAPS

Not only is the chicken hot and crunchy inside these wraps, but grilling the finished wraps also creates a fabulous crunch on the outside as well. These are extra ooey and gooey since they use fresh mozzarella. (Yes, you can substitute standard mozzarella, but give the fresh version a try!)

SERVES: 4
PREP TIME: 9 minutes
COOK TIME: 21 minutes
TOTAL TIME: 30 minutes

Ingredients

1 (25-ounce) bag frozen fully cooked crispy chicken strips

2 cubes frozen crushed garlic

4 cubes frozen chopped basil

1 tablespoon extra-virgin olive oil

½ cup freshly grated Parmesan cheese

½ teaspoon kosher salt

¼ teaspoon ground black pepper

4 (12") flatbread wraps

1 cup prepared marinara sauce

1 (8-ounce) ball fresh mozzarella cheese, sliced

PER SERVING

Calories: 817
Fat: 59g
Protein: 61g
Sodium: 2,589mg

Fiber: 3g
Carbohydrates: 44g
Sugar: 5g

1. Preheat oven to 400°F. Grease a baking sheet with non-stick spray.

2. Place chicken on prepared baking sheet. Bake until hot, about 15–17 minutes.

3. Heat a large skillet over high heat. In a small bowl, mash together garlic, basil, oil, Parmesan, salt, and pepper. Spread mixture onto each of the wraps. Top each wrap with about 2 pieces chicken, ¼ cup marinara, and one-fourth of the mozzarella slices.

4. To close each wrap, tuck in the ends first, then roll up tightly. Place seam-side down on the hot skillet and cook until golden brown, about 3 minutes. Flip and cook another 3 minutes. Serve.

BISCUIT-TOPPED CHICKEN POT PIE

This classic comfort food dish is a favorite with people young and old. The tops of the biscuits are crisp, while the bottoms act more like a dumpling since they bake in the gravy. This pie likes to bubble up and over the edges, so be sure you use a baking sheet under the pie to keep your oven clean.

SERVES: 6
PREP TIME: 4 minutes
COOK TIME: 26 minutes
TOTAL TIME: 30 minutes

Ingredients

⅓ cup salted butter

2 cubes frozen crushed garlic

1 cup frozen chopped onions

1 cup frozen sliced white mushrooms

1 medium stalk celery, diced

1¼ teaspoons kosher salt, divided

⅓ cup all-purpose flour

1¾ cups chicken broth

¼ cup heavy cream

1 cup frozen peas and carrots blend

2½ cups frozen fully cooked diced chicken breasts

½ teaspoon ground black pepper

8 frozen uncooked biscuits

PER SERVING

Calories: 432
Fat: 20g
Protein: 22g
Sodium: 1,791mg

Fiber: 2g
Carbohydrates: 39g
Sugar: 5g

1. Preheat oven to 400°F. Grease a 9" pie pan with non-stick spray.

2. Heat a large skillet over high heat. When hot, add butter, garlic, onions, mushrooms, celery, and ½ teaspoon salt. Sauté until vegetables soften, about 3–4 minutes.

3. Add flour and stir into the vegetables. The mixture will be very thick, but continue to cook for 1 minute, then add broth. Stir to incorporate flour into broth. Bring to a gentle boil, then add cream, peas and carrots, chicken, remaining ¾ teaspoon salt, and pepper. Cook for 2 minutes, then pour into the pie pan. Top with frozen biscuits.

4. Place pie pan on a baking sheet and bake until biscuits are done, about 20 minutes. Serve immediately.

CREAMY CHICKEN NOODLE SOUP

When it's snowy and frigid outside, you can't beat a hot pot of homemade chicken noodle soup for dinner. However, instead of simmering for hours, this soup comes together in only 30 minutes. This recipe cooks the noodles directly in the broth, which creates a smooth, creamy texture as the starch of the noodles releases into the soup. If you're looking to up your veggie game even more, toss in some frozen peas, peppers, or spinach.

SERVES: 6
PREP TIME: 10 minutes
COOK TIME: 20 minutes
TOTAL TIME: 30 minutes

Ingredients

2 tablespoons salted butter

1½ cups frozen onions

4 cubes frozen crushed garlic

1 cup frozen sliced white mushrooms

1 cup frozen sliced carrots

2 medium stalks celery, chopped

1 teaspoon kosher salt

½ teaspoon ground black pepper

10 cups chicken broth

1 (24-ounce) bag frozen egg noodles

1 (22-ounce) bag frozen fully cooked diced chicken breast

¼ cup heavy cream

1. Heat a large pot over high heat and add butter, onions, garlic, mushrooms, carrots, celery, salt, and pepper. Sauté for 2 minutes and add broth. Cover and bring to a boil.

2. Add noodles to pot and boil until al dente, around 18 minutes. Stir a few times while noodles cook to keep them from sticking to the bottom of the pot. Turn off heat, add frozen chicken and cream, and let sit for 2 minutes to allow chicken to heat up. Serve.

PER SERVING

Calories: 582	Fiber: 3g
Fat: 14g	Carbohydrates: 72g
Protein: 39g	Sugar: 7g
Sodium: 2,734mg	

GRILLED ITALIAN CHICKEN PANINIS

Before grilling the ciabatta rolls until they are all hot and crusty, we load them up with a winning combination of pesto, chicken, prosciutto, grilled onions, roasted peppers, and provolone cheese. If you don't have a panini press, use an electric skillet or a nonstick pan on the stove. Just add some weight to the tops of the sandwiches so they can compact like a true panini and get that authentic crispy crust. (You can cover them with a cookie sheet with a few heavy cans on top to press them flatter.)

SERVES: 4
PREP TIME: 10 minutes
COOK TIME: 10 minutes
TOTAL TIME: 20 minutes

Ingredients

½ tablespoon salted butter

1½ cups frozen chopped onions

¼ teaspoon kosher salt

10 ounces frozen fully cooked grilled chicken strips

½ cup prepared pesto

4 ciabatta rolls

8 (1-ounce) slices provolone cheese

8 slices prosciutto

⅓ cup roasted red pepper slices

PER SERVING

Calories: 750
Fat: 36g
Protein: 46g
Sodium: 2,132mg

Fiber: 3g
Carbohydrates: 60g
Sugar: 5g

1. Preheat a panini press to high. Heat a large skillet over high heat, then add butter, onions, and salt. Sauté on high for 5 minutes until onions brown. Set aside.

2. Heat chicken in microwave according to package directions. Set aside.

3. For each panini, spread 2 tablespoons pesto inside a roll and place 1 slice provolone on the top and bottom halves. Add 2 slices prosciutto and ¼ of the chicken to the bottom half of each. Finish off with grilled onions, 2–3 pepper slices, and top half of the bun. Cook in panini press until brown and crusty, about 5 minutes. Serve immediately.

ITALIAN WEDDING SOUP

Tender chicken meatballs are the star of this classic soup. Though it is broth-based, it's very hearty since it is full of vegetables and orzo pasta as well. If you prefer, you could use ground turkey in the meatballs instead of chicken.

SERVES: 8
PREP TIME: 10 minutes
COOK TIME: 20 minutes
TOTAL TIME: 30 minutes

Ingredients

1 pound ground chicken

½ cup panko bread crumbs

1 large egg, beaten

1½ cups frozen chopped onions, divided

7 cubes frozen crushed garlic, divided

½ cup freshly grated Parmesan cheese

2 teaspoons Italian seasoning

1 teaspoon kosher salt

½ teaspoon ground black pepper

2 (32-ounce) boxes chicken broth

1½ cups frozen sliced carrots

1½ cups frozen chopped spinach

1 cup uncooked orzo pasta

PER SERVING

Calories: 264
Fat: 7g
Protein: 19g
Sodium: 1,365mg
Fiber: 3g
Carbohydrates: 29g
Sugar: 4g

1. Preheat oven to 425°F. Grease a rimmed baking sheet with nonstick spray.

2. In a medium bowl, mix together chicken, bread crumbs, egg, ½ cup onions, 2 cubes garlic, Parmesan, Italian seasoning, salt, and pepper. (Mashing mixture with your hands works best to get it very well combined.) Use a 1½" cookie scoop to form twenty-five meatballs; arrange on the prepared baking sheet. Bake until cooked through, about 18 minutes.

3. While meatballs bake, in a large pot, combine broth, carrots, spinach, remaining 1 cup onions, and remaining 5 cubes garlic; cover. Bring to a boil over high heat, then add the orzo. Cook for 9 minutes, then add meatballs before serving.

JERK CHICKEN WITH BASIL MANGO SALSA

If you've ever been to Jamaica, you are already familiar with the delicious flavors of jerk chicken. Warm and spicy seasonings coat the outside of the meat while the mango salsa provides a sweet freshness to every bite. The heat level in this recipe's seasoning mix is on the milder end, so feel free to increase or decrease the amount of cayenne pepper to match your personal tastes. If you would like, some steamed rice makes a perfect side!

SERVES: 4
PREP TIME: 10 minutes
COOK TIME: 10 minutes
TOTAL TIME: 20 minutes

Ingredients

1 (22-ounce) bag frozen fully cooked grilled chicken breast strips

¾ teaspoon garlic powder

¾ teaspoon paprika

½ teaspoon ground cayenne pepper

¾ teaspoon cinnamon

¾ teaspoon allspice

1 teaspoon kosher salt, divided

1 (1-pound) bag frozen chopped mango

½ medium jalapeño pepper, cored, seeded, and finely diced

2 medium green onions, trimmed and chopped

¼ cup chopped fresh cilantro

2 cubes frozen chopped basil

2 tablespoons apple cider vinegar

1. Heat a large nonstick skillet over medium heat. When hot, add chicken, garlic powder, paprika, cayenne, cinnamon, allspice, and ½ teaspoon salt. Stir and heat until chicken is warm, about 5 minutes.

2. In a medium microwave-safe bowl, microwave mango at 20 percent power in 1-minute increments. Stir between each increment. Depending on your microwave's wattage, it will take 4–5 times to thaw mango. Chop thawed mango into smaller pieces and return to bowl. Add jalapeño, onions, cilantro, basil, vinegar, and remaining ½ teaspoon salt. Toss to combine.

3. Serve hot chicken with a generous scoop of mango salsa over the top.

PER SERVING

Calories: 281	Fiber: 3g
Fat: 6g	Carbohydrates: 23g
Protein: 37g	Sugar: 18g
Sodium: 1,419mg	

CHICKEN TACOS WITH MANGO JICAMA SALSA

These tacos are a light, healthy dinner that is quick enough to throw together on a busy weeknight. The warm spices of the chicken are balanced by the refreshing mango jicama salsa. If you aren't familiar with jicama, it is sold in the produce section of your grocery store and looks like a large round potato. You need to peel off the skin before using. Jicama is sweet and crisp, and might even become one of your favorite vegetables to eat raw!

SERVES: 8
PREP TIME: 10 minutes
COOK TIME: 10 minutes
TOTAL TIME: 20 minutes

Ingredients

¾ cup frozen chopped mango

¾ cup peeled and chopped jicama

1¼ cups frozen chopped onions, divided

1 teaspoon granulated sugar

1 tablespoon chopped fresh cilantro

1 tablespoon lime juice

½ teaspoon kosher salt, divided

¼ teaspoon ground black pepper, divided

1 (22-ounce) bag frozen fully cooked grilled chicken breast strips

1 cup frozen chopped green bell peppers

¾ teaspoon chili powder

¾ teaspoon ground cumin

8 (6") flour tortillas

1. In a medium microwave-safe bowl, microwave mango at 20 percent power in 1-minute increments. Stir between each increment. Depending on your microwave's wattage, it will take 4–5 times to thaw mango. Chop thawed mango into smaller pieces and return to bowl. Add jicama, ¼ cup frozen onions, sugar, cilantro, lime juice, ¼ teaspoon salt, and ⅛ teaspoon black pepper. Mix well and set aside.

2. Heat a large nonstick skillet over high heat. When hot, add chicken, green peppers, remaining 1 cup onions, chili powder, cumin, remaining ¼ teaspoon salt, and remaining ⅛ teaspoon black pepper. Cook until vegetables soften and chicken is hot, about 5 minutes.

3. Warm tortillas in the microwave for 30 seconds, then assemble with the chicken mixture topped with the mango salsa. Serve immediately.

PER SERVING

Calories: 218	Fiber: 2g
Fat: 5g	Carbohydrates: 24g
Protein: 21g	Sugar: 6g
Sodium: 787mg	

ASIAN NAPA CABBAGE SALAD

The ramen noodles might seem like an unorthodox ingredient in this salad, but they are an important part of the incredible crunchy topping. If you won't be eating the full salad in one sitting, only dress as much as you need. The salad will wilt after it has been dressed for too long.

SERVES: 6
PREP TIME: 15 minutes
COOK TIME: 5 minutes
TOTAL TIME: 20 minutes

Salad

1 (20-ounce) bag frozen fully cooked pulled chicken breast

2 tablespoons salted butter

1 cup slivered almonds

1 (3-ounce) package chicken-flavored ramen noodles, broken into small pieces

1 large head (3–4 pounds) napa cabbage, chopped

8 medium green onions, trimmed and chopped

Dressing

⅓ cup seasoned rice vinegar

6 tablespoons granulated sugar

1½ tablespoons soy sauce

1½ tablespoons sesame oil

⅓ cup canola oil

PER SERVING

Calories: 582	Fiber: 8g
Fat: 34g	Carbohydrates: 46g
Protein: 31g	Sugar: 26g
Sodium: 1,816mg	

1. To make the salad, in a medium microwave-safe bowl, heat chicken in 45-second increments until it thaws, about 4 minutes. Set aside.

2. In a medium skillet over medium heat, melt butter, then add almonds. Stir and cook until almonds begin to get a touch of color, 1–2 minutes, then add ramen noodle pieces. Continue to stir until almonds are evenly browned, about 3–4 minutes. Transfer to a medium bowl. Sprinkle ramen seasoning packet over almonds and noodles and stir to coat. Set aside.

3. To make the dressing, in a small bowl, whisk together all of the dressing ingredients. Set aside.

4. In a large salad bowl, combine cabbage, onions, chicken, and dressing. Toss to completely coat all ingredients, then top with ramen mixture. Serve immediately.

GARLIC BUTTER CAULIFLOWER PIZZA

Did you know that your grocer's freezer section carries a healthy cauliflower pizza crust ready to be topped however you like? Cauliflower crusts come out of the oven supercrisp and are the perfect canvas for this recipe, which is brimming with chicken, spinach, garlic, onions, and tomatoes. If you are following a low-carb diet, this pizza recipe will become your new favorite dinner!

SERVES: 4
PREP TIME: 5 minutes
COOK TIME: 15 minutes
TOTAL TIME: 20 minutes

Ingredients

2 (10") frozen cauliflower pizza crusts

2 tablespoons salted butter

3 cubes frozen crushed garlic

½ cup frozen chopped onions

½ cup frozen chopped spinach

¾ teaspoon kosher salt, divided

¼ teaspoon ground black pepper

1 medium Roma tomato, cored and chopped

3 tablespoons freshly grated Parmesan cheese

5 ounces fresh mozzarella cheese, thinly sliced

⅔ cup frozen fully cooked diced chicken breast

1. Preheat oven to 425°F. Place pizza crusts on baking sheets.

2. Heat a medium skillet over medium-high heat. When hot, add butter, garlic, onions, spinach, ½ teaspoon salt, and pepper. Cook just enough for vegetables to soften slightly, about 2 minutes. Spread mixture over pizza crusts.

3. Top pizzas with tomato, Parmesan, and mozzarella slices. Finish each pizza with frozen chicken, and sprinkle with remaining ¼ teaspoon salt. Bake until cheese is melted and crust is crispy, 13–15 minutes. Serve warm.

PER SERVING

Calories: 380
Fat: 21g
Protein: 19g
Sodium: 1,186mg

Fiber: 2g
Carbohydrates: 49g
Sugar: 3g

CHICKEN LO MEIN

These noodles are complemented by a bevy of vegetables, chicken, and an authentic Asian sauce. This recipe definitely hits the spot when you are craving takeout, and this version will taste even better. If you want more veggies, you could add some bean sprouts, pea pods, or julienned carrots at the same time as the peppers and onions.

SERVES: 4
PREP TIME: 5 minutes
COOK TIME: 16 minutes
TOTAL TIME: 21 minutes

Ingredients

¾ teaspoon kosher salt

8 ounces uncooked spaghetti

2 tablespoons soy sauce

1¼ teaspoons oyster sauce

2 teaspoons granulated sugar

1 teaspoon toasted sesame oil

½ teaspoon sriracha

1 tablespoon vegetable oil

2 cubes frozen crushed ginger

2 cubes frozen crushed garlic

1 cup frozen sliced white mushrooms

2 cups thinly sliced napa cabbage

2 cups frozen pepper and onion blend

2 cups frozen fully cooked grilled chicken breast strips

1. In a medium pot, bring 2 quarts water to a boil. Add salt and spaghetti. Cook for 9 minutes and drain.

2. While pasta is cooking, in a small bowl, mix soy sauce, oyster sauce, sugar, sesame oil, and sriracha. Set aside.

3. Heat a large skillet over high heat. When hot, add vegetable oil, ginger, garlic, mushrooms, and cabbage. Sauté for 3 minutes, then add peppers and onions and chicken. Cook for another 4–5 minutes. Add soy sauce mixture and cooked spaghetti, then toss to combine. Serve warm.

PER SERVING

Calories: 426
Fat: 8g
Protein: 30g
Sodium: 1,293mg

Fiber: 5g
Carbohydrates: 56g
Sugar: 9g

Chapter Five

BEEF AND PORK MAIN DISHES

THIS CHAPTER CONTAINS RECIPES THAT UTILIZE BOTH FRESH BEEF AND PORK AS WELL AS FROZEN PRECOOKED VERSIONS. EITHER WAY, THE PROMISE OF A 30-MINUTE PREP TIME REMAINS, ALONG WITH SOME FUN GLOBAL CULINARY ADVENTURES. LET YOUR TASTE BUDS TRAVEL TO LOCATIONS LIKE ASIA, THE MEDITERRANEAN, ITALY, AND MEXICO WHILE ENJOYING THE DEPTH OF FLAVOR AND SAVORY UMAMI TASTE THAT BEEF AND PORK ARE KNOWN FOR. IF YOU'RE IN THE MOOD FOR SOMETHING MORE BASIC, YOU'LL FIND SEVERAL TRADITIONAL AMERICAN RECIPES AS WELL.

CREAMY SPINACH PORK CHOPS

This unique take on pork chops is drenched in a rich and velvety sauce. Serve this recipe with a side of steamed vegetables or rice because you'll want to spoon this sauce over more than just those finished pork chops!

SERVES: 4
PREP TIME: 5 minutes
COOK TIME: 20 minutes
TOTAL TIME: 25 minutes

Ingredients

4 thick-cut boneless pork loin chops (about 2 pounds)

1½ teaspoons kosher salt, divided

¾ teaspoon ground black pepper, divided

1 teaspoon paprika

2 tablespoons salted butter, divided

6 cubes frozen crushed garlic

1 cup frozen chopped onions

2 tablespoons all-purpose flour

1½ cups 1% milk

¼ cup heavy cream

2 cups frozen chopped spinach

¼ cup freshly grated Parmesan cheese

½ teaspoon Italian seasoning

1. Preheat oven to 400°F.

2. Season chops with 1 teaspoon salt, ½ teaspoon pepper, and paprika.

3. Heat a large ovenproof skillet over high heat. When hot, add 1 tablespoon butter and chops. Cook until brown and meat releases from the surface of the skillet, about 3 minutes. Flip and cook another 3 minutes. Place skillet in oven and bake until internal temperature reaches 145°F, about 8 minutes.

4. Remove chops from skillet and return skillet to stove over medium-high heat. Add remaining 1 tablespoon butter, garlic, and onions. Sauté for 2 minutes, then add flour. Cook for 1 minute before adding milk and cream. Stir and allow sauce to thicken, about 2–3 minutes, before adding remaining ½ teaspoon salt, remaining ¼ teaspoon pepper, spinach, Parmesan, and Italian seasoning. Cook 1–2 minutes, then return chops to sauce and serve.

PER SERVING

Calories: 533
Fat: 22g
Protein: 60g
Sodium: 1,319mg

Fiber: 3g
Carbohydrates: 17g
Sugar: 7g

POT STICKER SOUP

This recipe transforms a classic appetizer into a mouthwatering soup. While the prep work only takes a few minutes, you will have to wait a bit longer for the pot stickers to finish cooking in the broth before diving in. Carrots, edamame, or pea pods would all be delicious additions to the soup, and would complement the hearty mushroom-flavored broth.

SERVES: 5
PREP TIME: 5 minutes
COOK TIME: 15 minutes
TOTAL TIME: 20 minutes

1. In a large pot over high heat, combine broth, mushrooms, onions, soy sauce, and pepper. Bring to a boil.

2. Add pot stickers and cook for 8 minutes. Add spinach, cook 1–2 minutes, and serve.

Ingredients

6 cups chicken broth

1 cup frozen sliced white mushrooms

3 medium green onions, trimmed and chopped

1 tablespoon soy sauce

½ teaspoon ground black pepper

20 frozen pork pot stickers

1 cup frozen chopped spinach

PER SERVING

Calories: 245
Fat: 7g
Protein: 14g
Sodium: 1,767mg

Fiber: 3g
Carbohydrates: 31g
Sugar: 5g

GREEK MEATBALL WRAPS WITH TZATZIKI SAUCE

Warm naan flatbread makes the perfect blanket around these bundles of meatballs, fresh vegetables, and a generous slather of garlicky tzatziki sauce. If dill isn't your favorite flavor, you can substitute parsley, mint, or thyme and still have a remarkable sauce for your wraps. If you are supershort on time, you can cheat this recipe by heating the meatballs in the microwave (according to package directions) instead of the oven.

SERVES: 4
PREP TIME: 10 minutes
COOK TIME: 15 minutes
TOTAL TIME: 25 minutes

Ingredients

40 frozen meatballs
   (about ⅔ of a 2-pound bag)

1 cup plain Greek yogurt

¼ cup grated cucumber

2 cubes frozen crushed garlic

2 teaspoons lemon juice

1 teaspoon extra-virgin olive oil

¼ teaspoon dried dill

1 teaspoon kosher salt, divided

1 teaspoon ground black pepper, divided

1 cup diced cucumber

1 cup diced tomatoes

1 cup thinly sliced red onion

4 (8") naan flatbreads

1. Preheat oven to 375°F. Place meatballs in single layer on a rimmed ungreased baking sheet and bake until hot, about 15 minutes.

2. In a small bowl, mix together yogurt, grated cucumber, garlic, lemon juice, oil, dill, ½ teaspoon salt, and ½ teaspoon pepper. Set aside.

3. In a medium bowl, toss together diced cucumber, tomatoes, onion, remaining ½ teaspoon salt, and remaining ½ teaspoon pepper. Set aside.

4. During the last 2 minutes of the meatballs' baking time, lay flatbreads on the other oven rack to warm. When meatballs are finished, remove everything from the oven. Assemble each wrap with 10 meatballs plus a generous helping of tzatziki and vegetables. Serve immediately.

PER SERVING

Calories: 877
Fat: 45g
Protein: 42g
Sodium: 2,275mg

Fiber: 8g
Carbohydrates: 69g
Sugar: 15g

ISLAND PORK CHOPS WITH MANGO AND BLACK BEANS

If you love Caribbean flavors, add all of these ingredients to your shopping list now! The warm spices rubbed into the pork and the spiciness of the black beans are mellowed by a refreshing mango salsa. The one perfect bite includes a bit of all three on your fork at the same time. Now all you need is your favorite tropical drink and a white sandy beach to complete the dream.

SERVES: 4
PREP TIME: 5 minutes
COOK TIME: 25 minutes
TOTAL TIME: 30 minutes

Ingredients

1⅛ teaspoons kosher salt, divided

1 teaspoon chili powder

1 teaspoon smoked paprika

4 thick-cut boneless pork loin chops (about 2 pounds)

2 teaspoons vegetable oil

Juice of 1½ medium oranges, divided

3 slices thick-cut bacon, chopped small

2 cubes frozen crushed garlic, divided

½ medium jalapeño pepper, cored, seeded, and finely diced

1 (15-ounce) can black beans, drained and rinsed

½ cup water

2 cups frozen chopped mango

1½ tablespoons chopped fresh cilantro

Juice of ½ medium lime

1. Preheat oven to 400°F.

2. In a small dish, mix together 1 teaspoon salt with chili powder and paprika. Rub spices on both sides of the chops.

3. Heat a large ovenproof skillet over high heat. When hot, add oil, then pork chops. Cook until they brown and release from the surface of the skillet, about 3 minutes. Flip and repeat on the second side. Add juice of 1 orange over the top, then place skillet in the oven. Bake chops until their interiors reach 145°F, about 8 minutes. Remove and let chops rest 5 minutes.

4. In a small skillet over high heat, cook bacon until crisp, about 3–4 minutes; then add 1 cube garlic and jalapeño Cook for 2 minutes before adding black beans and water. Simmer for 3 minutes.

5. In a medium microwave-safe bowl, microwave mango at 20 percent power in 1-minute increments. Stir between each increment. Depending on your microwave's wattage, it will take 4–5 times to thaw mango. Chop thawed mango into smaller pieces and return to the bowl. Add cilantro, lime juice, remaining juice of ½ orange, remaining ⅛ teaspoon salt, and remaining 1 cube garlic. Mix well.

6. Plate each pork chop and top with the black beans and mango salsa. Serve immediately.

PER SERVING

Calories: 651	Fiber: 9g
Fat: 29g	Carbohydrates: 33g
Protein: 58g	Sugar: 14g
Sodium: 1,191mg	

SWISS MUSHROOM STEAK HOAGIES

The classic combo of beef with Swiss cheese and sautéed mushrooms is the star of these toasted sub rolls. The juices from the filling soak into the bread on the inside, but the rolls stay perfectly crunchy on the outside. If you are looking for more of a Philly cheesesteak flavor profile, substitute green bell peppers for the mushrooms and use provolone cheese instead of Swiss.

SERVES: 6
PREP TIME: 10 minutes
COOK TIME: 17 minutes
TOTAL TIME: 27 minutes

Ingredients

2 tablespoons salted butter

1½ cups frozen chopped onions

1½ cups frozen sliced white mushrooms

4 cubes frozen crushed garlic

¾ teaspoon kosher salt

½ teaspoon ground black pepper

1 (16-ounce) bag frozen fully cooked steak strips

4 teaspoons Worcestershire sauce

1 teaspoon cornstarch

2 teaspoons water

6 hoagie rolls

6 (1-ounce) slices Swiss cheese

1. Preheat oven to 400°F.

2. Heat a large skillet over high heat. When hot, add butter, onions, mushrooms, garlic, salt, and pepper. Sauté until vegetables soften, about 3–4 minutes.

3. Add steak strips and Worcestershire to the skillet, then continue to cook until beef heats through, about 5 minutes. In a small cup, combine cornstarch with water and add to the meat. Stir and cook until sauce thickens slightly, about 1 minute.

4. Divide filling among rolls, top with Swiss, and bake on an ungreased baking sheet until cheese melts and exterior of rolls becomes crispy, about 8 minutes. Serve immediately.

PER SERVING

Calories: 489

Fat: 20g

Protein: 36g

Sodium: 1,121mg

Fiber: 3g

Carbohydrates: 43g

Sugar: 6g

MEATBALL AND MOZZARELLA STICK SUBS

Meatball subs are delicious all on their own—but wait till you try them with hot mozzarella sticks on top! A schmear of pesto on the inside of the sub rolls provides a surprising freshness to the sandwich. If you want to go for a showstopping presentation, make one big sub with a full loaf of Italian or French bread from the bakery. That's how you wow the crowd at your next big game feast!

SERVES: 6
PREP TIME: 10 minutes
COOK TIME: 20 minutes
TOTAL TIME: 30 minutes

Ingredients

24 frozen Italian meatballs

12 frozen breaded mozzarella sticks

6 tablespoons prepared pesto

6 (5") hoagie rolls

¾ cup prepared marinara sauce

6 slices provolone cheese, cut in half

PER SERVING

Calories: 769
Fat: 43g
Protein: 35g
Sodium: 1,716mg

Fiber: 5g
Carbohydrates: 61g
Sugar: 8g

1. Preheat oven to 425°F.

2. Place meatballs and mozzarella sticks on rimmed baking sheet and bake for 12 minutes.

3. Spread 1 tablespoon pesto inside each roll. Add 4 meatballs, 2 tablespoons marinara, 2 slices provolone, then 2 mozzarella sticks to each sub. Place on baking sheet and bake until cheese melts and rolls get crusty, about 8 minutes. Serve immediately.

ITALIAN TORTELLINI SALAD

Tired of boring pasta salads? Try this variation! Using frozen cheese tortellini in pasta salads adds more flavor and heartiness to every serving. The finished bowl is brimming with vegetables, salami, and fresh mozzarella cheese. Plus, the quick homemade Italian salad dressing is the perfect finish. If you would like to increase the protein in this salad, some diced cooked chicken would be a delicious addition.

SERVES: 4
PREP TIME: 15 minutes
COOK TIME: 5 minutes
TOTAL TIME: 20 minutes

Pasta Salad

1 teaspoon kosher salt

1 (20-ounce) bag frozen uncooked cheese tortellini

1 medium cucumber, diced

2 medium Roma tomatoes, cored and diced

1 medium red or yellow bell pepper, cored, seeded, and diced

4 ounces fresh mozzarella cheese, diced

4 ounces salami, diced

15 black olives, sliced

15 slices peperoncini, chopped

Dressing

1 cube frozen crushed garlic

3 tablespoons red wine vinegar

1 teaspoon Italian seasoning

1 teaspoon kosher salt

¼ cup extra-virgin olive oil

1. To make the salad, in a medium pot over high heat, bring 2 quarts water to a boil. Add 1 teaspoon salt and tortellini. Cook for 3 minutes. Drain and rinse with cold water. Set aside.

2. In a large bowl, add cucumber, tomatoes, bell pepper, mozzarella, salami, olives, peperoncini, and tortellini.

3. To make the dressing, in a small bowl, mash garlic with vinegar. Add Italian seasoning and salt. Whisk in oil. Pour dressing over salad and toss to combine. Serve immediately.

PER SERVING

Calories: 572
Fat: 33g
Protein: 28g
Sodium: 2,118mg

Fiber: 10g
Carbohydrates: 60g
Sugar: 5g

CHEESY GROUND BEEF NACHO CASSEROLE

This substantial nacho bake presents layers of tortilla chips loaded with ground beef, black beans, corn, and cheese. It's a crowd pleaser, featuring many favorite flavors. This recipe uses green enchilada sauce, but feel free to use red if you prefer. Also, you could assemble this dish earlier in the day, keep it covered in the refrigerator until you are ready, and then bake it. Just add a few extra minutes to your baking time.

SERVES: 8
PREP TIME: 5 minutes
COOK TIME: 25 minutes
TOTAL TIME: 30 minutes

Ingredients

1 pound 85/15 ground beef

1 teaspoon kosher salt

½ teaspoon ground black pepper

2 cubes frozen crushed garlic

1 (15-ounce) can petite diced tomatoes, drained

2 (15-ounce) cans black beans, drained and rinsed

1½ cups frozen corn

1 (28-ounce) can green enchilada sauce

1 (12-ounce) bag corn tortilla chips

3 cups (12 ounces) shredded Cheddar cheese

1 medium avocado, peeled, pitted, and diced

½ cup sour cream

PER SERVING

Calories: 733
Fat: 36g
Protein: 32g
Sodium: 1,483mg

Fiber: 12g
Carbohydrates: 63g
Sugar: 5g

1. Preheat oven to 450°F. Grease a 9" × 13" pan with non-stick spray.

2. In a large skillet over high heat, cook ground beef with salt, pepper, and garlic until meat is no longer pink, about 5 minutes. Add tomatoes, black beans, and corn.

3. Spread a thin layer of enchilada sauce evenly in the prepared pan, then lay down one-third of the tortilla chips, using your hands to crush them a bit. Top chips with half the meat mixture, then half the Cheddar and one-third of the enchilada sauce. Repeat this layering one more time.

4. Top casserole with the remaining chips and enchilada sauce. Bake uncovered until the casserole is bubbly along the edges of the pan, about 20 minutes. Serve with diced avocado and sour cream.

STEAK FAJITA BURRITO BOWLS WITH PICO DE GALLO

This quick dinner is packed with protein, whole grains, veggies, and your favorite Southwestern flavors! While the fresh lime juice might seem like an unnecessary garnish, don't skip that small addition at the end, because it brightens and enhances every flavor in the bowl.

SERVES: 4
PREP TIME: 15 minutes
COOK TIME: 7 minutes
TOTAL TIME: 22 minutes

Pico de Gallo

1 pound tomatoes, cored and diced

½ medium red onion, peeled and diced

1 medium jalapeño pepper, seeded, cored, and minced

1 bunch fresh cilantro, chopped

Juice of 1 medium lime

¾ teaspoon kosher salt

¼ teaspoon ground black pepper

Burrito Bowls

2 (10-ounce) bags frozen brown rice

1 (16-ounce) bag frozen fully cooked seasoned steak strips

1 (20-ounce) bag frozen pepper and onion blend

3 tablespoons fajita seasoning mix

1 (15-ounce) can black beans, drained and rinsed

1 cup (4 ounces) shredded Cheddar cheese

2 medium avocados, peeled, pitted, and diced

Juice of 1 medium lime

1. To make the pico de gallo, in a medium bowl, combine tomatoes, onion, jalapeño, cilantro, lime juice, salt, and pepper. Set aside.

2. To make the burrito bowls, follow directions on the package to heat the rice in the microwave. Set aside.

3. Heat a large skillet over high heat. When hot, add frozen steak and cook for 2 minutes. Add peppers and onions. Continue to cook for 5 minutes until vegetables are heated through, then add fajita seasoning. Mix well.

4. While meat is cooking, in a medium microwave-safe bowl, microwave beans on high for 2 minutes.

5. To assemble the bowls, layer rice, steak, and beans in each bowl. Top with Cheddar, avocado, and pico de gallo. Finish with a squeeze of fresh lime juice and serve.

PER SERVING

Calories: 810	Fiber: 17g
Fat: 24g	Carbohydrates: 95g
Protein: 52g	Sugar: 6g
Sodium: 1,868mg	

TAQUITO SALAD WITH CILANTRO LIME RANCH DRESSING

This salad is quite substantial, loaded with beef taquitos, black beans, corn, tomatoes, avocado, cheese, and a semi-homemade dressing. (There's nothing wrong with taking a prepared product and adding your own spin to improve the flavor!) You could add some bacon, chicken, or olives to this salad to change up the flavor profile.

SERVES: 6
PREP TIME: 10 minutes
COOK TIME: 10 minutes
TOTAL TIME: 20 minutes

Salad

1 (23-ounce) box frozen beef taquitos

1½ cups frozen corn

3 medium romaine lettuce hearts, cored and chopped

1 (15-ounce) can black beans, drained and rinsed

2 medium Roma tomatoes, cored and chopped

6 medium green onions, trimmed and chopped

1 medium avocado, seeded, peeled, and diced

1 cup (4 ounces) shredded Cheddar cheese

Dressing

¾ cup prepared ranch dressing

½ cup fresh cilantro leaves

Juice of ½ medium lime

½ medium jalapeño pepper, cored and seeded

1. To make the salad, bake taquitos in the oven according to package directions. Chop into smaller pieces.

2. Place corn in mesh strainer and run under cold water for 3 minutes to thaw.

3. In a large bowl, layer lettuce, beans, corn, tomatoes, onions, avocado, Cheddar, and taquitos.

4. To make the dressing, place ranch dressing, cilantro, lime juice, and jalapeño in a blender. Blend on high until smooth.

5. Add dressing to salad and toss to combine. Serve immediately.

PER SERVING

Calories: 572
Fat: 19g
Protein: 22g
Sodium: 622mg

Fiber: 18g
Carbohydrates: 81g
Sugar: 6g

SESAME GINGER BEEF AND GREEN BEANS

Even if you love your favorite takeout place's version of this meal, making it at home will taste even better. Plus, your dinner will be done in less than 15 minutes, which makes it even faster than takeout. Double bonus! While a lot of Asian sauces are a bit heavy and sweet, this recipe uses just enough sugar along with a squeeze of lime juice to brighten the whole dish. You can serve this awesomeness on its own or with a side of steamed rice.

SERVES: 4
PREP TIME: 5 minutes
COOK TIME: 7 minutes
TOTAL TIME: 12 minutes

Ingredients

3 cubes frozen crushed garlic

3 cubes frozen crushed ginger

5 tablespoons soy sauce

1 teaspoon oyster sauce

¼ cup granulated sugar

2 tablespoons seasoned rice vinegar

1 tablespoon cornstarch

1 tablespoon vegetable oil

1 (16-ounce) bag frozen fully cooked steak strips

1 (10-ounce) bag frozen whole green beans

Juice of ½ medium lime

1 tablespoon sesame seeds

2 medium green onions, trimmed and chopped

1. In a small bowl, mash together garlic and ginger, then add soy and oyster sauces, sugar, vinegar, and cornstarch. Set aside.

2. Heat a large skillet over high heat. When hot, add oil, steak, and green beans. Cook until heated through, about 5 minutes. Add soy sauce mixture and mix together. Heat until sauce thickens, about 2 minutes, then add lime juice, sesame seeds, and onions. Stir and serve immediately.

PER SERVING

Calories: 314
Fat: 9g
Protein: 32g
Sodium: 2,139mg

Fiber: 3g
Carbohydrates: 27g
Sugar: 17g

BEEF TERIYAKI WRAPS

These wraps have a delicious sweetness thanks to the homemade teriyaki sauce and the pineapple. The sauce takes only a few minutes to make and is significantly better than the type you can buy at the store, which can be so sweet it overpowers any other flavor. You can add sliced tomatoes to your wrap if you like.

SERVES: 6
PREP TIME: 5 minutes
COOK TIME: 10 minutes
TOTAL TIME: 15 minutes

Ingredients

2 tablespoons soy sauce

2 tablespoons brown sugar

1 tablespoon honey

¼ teaspoon garlic powder

¼ teaspoon ground ginger

1½ teaspoons cornstarch

½ cup water

1 (16-ounce) bag frozen fully cooked steak strips

1½ cups frozen chopped pineapple

1½ cups frozen pepper and onion blend

6 flatbread wraps

1 medium head romaine lettuce, cored and separated into leaves

1 medium cucumber, sliced

1. In a small saucepan, combine soy sauce, brown sugar, honey, garlic powder, ginger, cornstarch, and water. Bring mixture to a simmer over high heat and thicken for about 2 minutes before removing from heat.

2. Heat a large nonstick skillet over high heat. When hot, add steak, pineapple, and peppers and onions. Sauté for 3 minutes, then add half the teriyaki sauce and continue to cook until everything is warm, about 5 more minutes.

3. Divide mixture among flatbreads, then add lettuce, cucumber, and any additional teriyaki sauce if desired. Serve immediately.

PER SERVING

Calories: 282	Fiber: 13g
Fat: 5g	Carbohydrates: 43g
Protein: 28g	Sugar: 14g
Sodium: 1,002mg	

ITALIAN PROSCIUTTO AND CANTALOUPE FLATBREAD

If you love a sweet and salty taste combination, this flatbread recipe will hit the spot. Pairing ripe cantaloupe, salty prosciutto, and a sweet balsamic drizzle may sound a bit odd, but as soon as you take that first delicious bite, you will be brainstorming so many different ways to use them in other recipes. The recipe uses a balsamic glaze, which you can find by the vinegar products at your store—or you can make your own by simmering balsamic vinegar over medium heat until it becomes a syrup.

SERVES: 4
PREP TIME: 5 minutes
COOK TIME: 11 minutes
TOTAL TIME: 16 minutes

Ingredients

2 (8") naan flatbreads

1 tablespoon extra-virgin olive oil

1½ cups frozen chopped onions

½ teaspoon kosher salt

¼ teaspoon ground black pepper

2 cubes frozen crushed garlic

2 cubes frozen chopped basil

¼ cup freshly grated Parmesan cheese

4 ounces fresh mozzarella cheese, sliced

3 ounces sliced prosciutto

½ cup very thinly sliced cantaloupe

2 tablespoons balsamic reduction glaze

PER SERVING

Calories: 285
Fat: 17g
Protein: 17g
Sodium: 834mg

Fiber: 2g
Carbohydrates: 32g
Sugar: 7g

1. Preheat oven to 400°F. Place flatbreads on rimmed baking sheet.

2. Heat a large skillet over high heat. When hot, add oil, onions, salt, and pepper. Cook until onions soften, about 3 minutes, then add garlic. Continue to cook until onions are browned, about 3–4 minutes. Turn off heat and add basil. Mix to incorporate basil into onions, then spread onto flatbreads.

3. Top flatbreads with Parmesan and mozzarella. Bake for 5 minutes. Remove and add prosciutto and cantaloupe; drizzle on balsamic glaze. Serve immediately.

CHILI CORN BREAD SKILLET

The corn bread that tops this slightly spicy chili is tender, moist, and lightly sweet. When it comes time to spoon the corn bread batter over the chili, you will think you've completely messed up this recipe because it just doesn't seem right. Shouldn't the batter be thicker? Why is it sinking? Trust the recipe and put it in the oven. When you open it up 15 minutes later, you'll wonder why you ever doubted your skills. This recipe uses an all-purpose baking mix like Bisquick or Jiffy baking mix.

SERVES: 6
PREP TIME: 8 minutes
COOK TIME: 22 minutes
TOTAL TIME: 30 minutes

Ingredients

½ pound 85/15 ground beef

¾ cup frozen chopped onions

2 cubes frozen crushed garlic

½ teaspoon kosher salt

1 (10-ounce) can diced tomatoes with chilies, drained

2 (15-ounce) cans chili beans

1 cup all-purpose baking mix

¼ cup cornmeal

¼ cup granulated sugar

1½ teaspoons baking powder

½ cup 1% milk

1 large egg

4 tablespoons salted butter, melted

1. Preheat oven to 400°F.

2. Spray a 12" oven-safe skillet with nonstick spray and heat over high heat. When hot, add beef, onions, garlic, and salt. Cook until meat is no longer pink, about 5 minutes. Add drained tomatoes and chili beans with their liquid. Bring to a full boil.

3. While chili is cooking, in a medium bowl, mix together baking mix, cornmeal, sugar, and baking powder. Add milk, egg, and melted butter. Mix together well and spoon evenly over the top of the chili. Do not mix or spread. Bake until corn bread is cooked and lightly brown on top, 15–18 minutes. Serve.

PER SERVING

Calories: 437
Fat: 14g
Protein: 19g
Sodium: 923mg

Fiber: 8g
Carbohydrates: 56g
Sugar: 15g

PHILLY CHEESESTEAK SLOPPY JOES

This is a delicious remake of the classic sloppy joe. This version has ground beef, onions, peppers, and mushrooms, surrounded by a heavenly provolone cheese sauce. These sandwiches would be a great option to bring to your next potluck, but be prepared to share the recipe because your friends will definitely be asking for it!

SERVES: 8
PREP TIME: 5 minutes
COOK TIME: 15 minutes
TOTAL TIME: 20 minutes

Ingredients

1 pound 85/15 ground beef

1¼ teaspoons kosher salt, divided

½ teaspoon ground black pepper

1½ cups frozen chopped onions

¾ cup frozen chopped green bell peppers

1 cup frozen sliced white mushrooms

2 cubes frozen crushed garlic

2 tablespoons ketchup

1 tablespoon Worcestershire sauce

1 cup beef broth

1 tablespoon cornstarch

8 ounces provolone cheese, chopped small

8 hamburger buns

1. Heat a large skillet over high heat. When hot, spray with nonstick spray, then add beef, ½ teaspoon salt, and black pepper. Cook until meat is no longer pink and any moisture has evaporated, about 7 minutes. Transfer meat to a bowl, leaving any grease in the skillet.

2. Return skillet to high heat and add onions, peppers, mushrooms, garlic, and ¼ teaspoon salt. Sauté until vegetables soften, about 3–4 minutes. Return beef to skillet, along with ketchup, Worcestershire sauce, and remaining ½ teaspoon salt. Stir.

3. Combine broth with cornstarch and add to the skillet. Cook until sauce thickens, about 2 minutes, then reduce heat to medium. Add provolone and stir to allow the cheese to completely melt. Serve on hamburger buns.

PER SERVING

Calories: 367	Fiber: 2g
Fat: 16g	Carbohydrates: 28g
Protein: 23g	Sugar: 6g
Sodium: 981mg	

Chapter Six

FISH AND SEAFOOD MAIN DISHES

IF YOU'RE USED TO ONLY COOKING FRESH SEAFOOD, GET READY TO EXPAND YOUR HORIZONS. FROZEN FISH WILL NOW BECOME YOUR GO-TO WHEN YOU'RE LOOKING TO COOK FLAVORFUL AND HEALTHY MEALS. DID YOU KNOW THAT PEOPLE WHO EAT FISH HAVE LOWER BLOOD PRESSURE AND FEWER HEART ATTACKS THAN THOSE WHO DON'T INCLUDE FISH IN THEIR DIET? LOADED WITH IMPORTANT OMEGA-3 FATTY ACIDS, A PROTEIN-RICH PIECE OF FISH ONCE A WEEK IS A FABULOUS WAY TO TAKE A STEP TOWARD A HEALTHIER LIFESTYLE.

BUYING FRESH FISH AND SHELLFISH CAN BE INTIMIDATING IF YOU DON'T KNOW THE PROPER CUES FOR FRESHNESS. LUCKILY, FROZEN SEAFOOD ABOUNDS AT YOUR LOCAL GROCERY STORE, SAFE AND READY TO USE FOR DINNER TONIGHT. NO, YOU DON'T NEED TO WAIT FOR IT TO THAW IN THE FRIDGE OVERNIGHT. IN FACT, I'M GOING TO TEACH YOU HOW TO COOK A FROZEN FILLET OF FISH WITHOUT ANY TYPE OF THAWING REQUIRED! THESE RECIPES WILL GIVE YOU ALL THE CONFIDENCE YOU NEED TO MAKE SEAFOOD A REGULAR PART OF YOUR MEAL PLAN.

FRIED FISH TACOS WITH CILANTRO LIME SLAW

These tacos will quickly become an all-time favorite with your family, thanks to the bright flavors. To warm corn tortillas, use a pair of tongs to hold them over the open flame of a gas stove and flip them around until they are slightly charred on the edges. That bit of char adds great flavor to your taco. You can substitute flour tortillas, but the sweetness of the corn creates a delicious balance with the tart slaw and the spice of the fish.

SERVES: 10
PREP TIME: 10 minutes
COOK TIME: 20 minutes
TOTAL TIME: 30 minutes

Ingredients

1 teaspoon chili powder

1 teaspoon ground cumin

1 teaspoon garlic powder

1½ teaspoons kosher salt, divided

1 (19-ounce) package frozen battered fish fillets

2½ cups thinly sliced cabbage

¾ cup thinly sliced red onion

¼ cup chopped fresh cilantro

1 medium jalapeño pepper, seeded, cored, and minced

Juice of 1 medium lime

2 teaspoons extra-virgin olive oil

10 corn tortillas

⅓ cup crumbled queso fresco

1 medium avocado, peeled, pitted, and sliced

1. Preheat oven to 450°F.

2. In a small bowl, combine chili powder, cumin, garlic powder, and 1 teaspoon salt. Rub mixture on the outside of fish fillets. Place on rimmed baking sheet and bake for 20 minutes, flipping fish over after 10 minutes.

3. In a medium bowl, combine cabbage and remaining ½ teaspoon salt. Add onion, cilantro, jalapeño, lime juice, and oil. Toss together and set aside for 10 minutes to allow the cabbage to begin to wilt.

4. To assemble finished tacos, heat corn tortillas and layer with one fish fillet, queso fresco, avocado, and slaw. Serve immediately.

PER SERVING

Calories: 256	*Fiber: 4g*
Fat: 12g	*Carbohydrates: 27g*
Protein: 9g	*Sugar: 2g*
Sodium: 619mg	

BAKED SHRIMP SCAMPI

This dish is completely stunning. The shrimp bake in a scrumptious lemon garlic sauce and are topped with a garlicky panko topping. Serve this dish with a side of rice or roasted potatoes. (Be sure to scoop some of the buttery pan juices out of the shrimp dish over your rice or potatoes!)

SERVES: 6
PREP TIME: 18 minutes
COOK TIME: 12 minutes
TOTAL TIME: 30 minutes

Ingredients

2 pounds (16–22 per pound) frozen raw peeled and deveined shrimp

3 tablespoons extra-virgin olive oil

1 tablespoon red wine vinegar

2 teaspoons kosher salt

1 teaspoon ground black pepper

8 tablespoons salted butter, at room temperature

4 cubes frozen crushed garlic

¼ cup minced green onions

3 tablespoons minced fresh flat-leaf Italian parsley

¼ teaspoon red pepper flakes

2 tablespoons lemon juice

1 teaspoon lemon zest

1 medium egg yolk

⅔ cup panko bread crumbs

1. Preheat oven to 425°F. Grease a 2-quart casserole dish with nonstick spray.

2. Place frozen shrimp in a large mesh strainer and place under cold running water for about 5 minutes to thaw. Stir shrimp around often to aid in the thawing process. Once thawed, butterfly each shrimp by running a knife down its back with the blade inserted about two-thirds of the way into the shrimp.

3. In a large bowl, toss shrimp with oil, vinegar, salt, and pepper. Arrange them cut-side down with the tails curling up in prepared casserole dish. Pour any liquid left in the bowl over the arranged shrimp.

4. In a small bowl, mix together butter, garlic, onions, parsley, red pepper flakes, lemon juice, lemon zest, egg yolk, and bread crumbs. Dot butter mixture evenly over shrimp and bake until hot and bubbly, about 12 minutes. Serve immediately.

PER SERVING

Calories: 439	Fiber: 0g
Fat: 25g	Carbohydrates: 14g
Protein: 38g	Sugar: 1g
Sodium: 2,218mg	

MANGO AND SHRIMP SUSHI BOWL WITH SOY GINGER SAUCE

This gorgeous bowl features five different frozen ingredients, which puts this meal on the fast track to the table without compromising flavor. The soy ginger sauce coats every bite with a delicious savory taste. There's no need to thaw the frozen crushed ginger and garlic because they are soft right from the freezer. Just mash them with a fork. Also, feel free to add some nori pieces or any of your favorite veggies, nuts, or seeds to personalize this dish.

SERVES: 4
PREP TIME: 20 minutes
COOK TIME: 5 minutes
TOTAL TIME: 25 minutes

Sushi Rice

1 (18-ounce) box frozen sticky white rice

4½ teaspoons seasoned rice vinegar

4½ teaspoons granulated sugar

1 teaspoon kosher salt

Toppings

1 (12-ounce) bag frozen fully cooked peeled and deveined medium shrimp

1 cup frozen chopped mango

½ medium English cucumber, diced

1 medium avocado, peeled, pitted, and diced

¼ cup prepared sriracha mayonnaise

Soy Ginger Sauce

2 cubes frozen crushed ginger

2 cubes frozen crushed garlic

½ cup soy sauce

¼ cup seasoned rice vinegar

2 teaspoons granulated sugar

1 teaspoon toasted sesame oil

Continued on next page

MANGO AND SHRIMP SUSHI BOWL WITH SOY GINGER SAUCE CONT.

1. To make the sushi rice, follow directions on the box to heat sticky rice. Set aside.

2. In a large microwave-safe bowl, combine vinegar, sugar, and salt. Microwave on high for 45 seconds. Stir, then add the hot rice. Use a rubber spatula to toss rice and seasoning mixture together.

3. Place bowl of rice in the freezer to cool to room temperature, approximately 15 minutes. Stir every 5 minutes to help it cool quicker.

4. While rice is cooking, make the toppings. Place frozen shrimp in a large mesh strainer under cold running water for about 5 minutes to thaw. Move shrimp around a few times to aid in the thawing process. Once thawed, remove tails and chop into bite-sized pieces. Set aside.

5. In a medium microwave-safe bowl, heat mango at 20 percent power for 1-minute increments. Stir between each increment. Depending on your microwave's power level, it will take 4–5 times to thaw the mango. Chop into smaller pieces and set aside.

6. To make the soy ginger sauce, in a small bowl, combine ginger, garlic, soy sauce, vinegar, sugar, and oil. Set aside.

7. To prepare finished bowls, evenly divide rice among four bowls and top with shrimp, mango, cucumber, and avocado. Drizzle 3–4 teaspoons soy ginger sauce per bowl, then add about 1 tablespoon sriracha mayonnaise, depending on how spicy you want your bowl. Serve immediately.

PER SERVING

Calories: 529
Fat: 18g
Protein: 28g
Sodium: 4,013mg

Fiber: 3g
Carbohydrates: 73g
Sugar: 23g

TUNA VEGGIE MAC AND CHEESE

Subbing out half of the pasta for cauliflower and broccoli in this mac and cheese makes eating vegetables fun! The garlicky cheese sauce is full-flavored without being overpowering. If your family doesn't like tuna, keep it in big chunks instead of flaking it up...they might think it is chicken.

SERVES: 6
PREP TIME: 10 minutes
COOK TIME: 20 minutes
TOTAL TIME: 30 minutes

Ingredients

2½ teaspoons kosher salt, divided

8 ounces uncooked penne pasta

2 (12-ounce) bags frozen cauliflower florets

1 (12-ounce) bag frozen broccoli florets

3 tablespoons salted butter

1½ cups frozen chopped onions

4 cubes frozen crushed garlic

3 tablespoons all-purpose flour

2½ cups 1% milk

¼ cup heavy cream

¾ teaspoon ground black pepper

2 cups (8 ounces) shredded sharp Cheddar cheese

¾ cup freshly grated Parmesan cheese

1 (6-ounce) can solid white albacore tuna in water, drained

1. In a large pot, bring 2 quarts water to a boil. Add 1 teaspoon salt and penne. Cook for 10 minutes, drain, and return to pot.

2. Cook cauliflower and broccoli in the microwave according to package directions. Drain any water from the bags and add vegetables to the penne.

3. Heat a large skillet over high heat. When hot, add butter, onions, and garlic. Sauté until onions soften, about 3 minutes. Add flour, mix well, and cook for 1 minute before adding milk, cream, remaining 1½ teaspoons salt, and pepper. Whisk well to combine flour with milk. Bring to a boil and allow sauce to thicken, about 3–5 minutes, before adding Cheddar and Parmesan. Mix and allow cheeses to melt.

4. Pour cheese sauce over pasta and add tuna. Toss to combine, and serve.

PER SERVING

Calories: 584
Fat: 25g
Protein: 32g
Sodium: 984mg

Fiber: 7g
Carbohydrates: 51g
Sugar: 11g

PARMESAN PANKO–CRUSTED COD

This divine fish recipe is only 261 calories per serving and looks as yummy as it tastes. Plus, there is absolutely no need to thaw the pieces of cod before baking them. Serve some freshly steamed green beans or broccoli on the side for a perfectly balanced dinner.

SERVES: 6
PREP TIME: 10 minutes
COOK TIME: 15 minutes
TOTAL TIME: 25 minutes

Ingredients

2 pounds frozen wild-caught Alaskan cod fillets

1⅛ teaspoons kosher salt, divided

¾ teaspoon ground black pepper, divided

3 tablespoons salted butter

2 cubes frozen crushed garlic

3 tablespoons chopped fresh flat-leaf parsley

½ cup freshly grated Parmesan cheese

1 cup panko bread crumbs

Zest and juice of 1 medium lemon

PER SERVING

Calories: 261
Fat: 9g
Protein: 28g
Sodium: 1,135mg

Fiber: 0g
Carbohydrates: 15g
Sugar: 1g

1. Preheat oven to 450°F. Lightly grease a large baking sheet with nonstick spray.

2. Remove fish from wrappers and rinse each piece in cold water for 30 seconds to remove any ice or frost on the surface. Pat dry with paper towels and lay on baking sheet. (Fish will still be frozen.) Season both sides of the fish with 1 teaspoon salt and ½ teaspoon pepper.

3. In a small microwave-safe bowl, combine butter and garlic, then microwave on high for 30 seconds until butter melts. Add parsley, Parmesan, bread crumbs, lemon zest, remaining ⅛ teaspoon salt, and remaining ¼ teaspoon pepper. Divide topping among the fillets, pressing down gently so it sticks. Bake until fish is mostly opaque, 15–17 minutes. Serve immediately with a small squeeze of lemon juice over the top of each piece.

CREAMY TUSCAN SKILLET SALMON

This pan-seared salmon is served smothered in a heavenly garlic cream sauce that is loaded with artichokes, sun-dried tomatoes, and spinach. You'll be transported straight to Italy when you taste these flavors together. If you are looking for a low-carb dinner, serve a nice salad or steamed vegetable on the side; if carbs aren't a concern for you, this fish is delightful over some steamed rice.

SERVES: 4
PREP TIME: 10 minutes
COOK TIME: 15 minutes
TOTAL TIME: 25 minutes

Ingredients

4 (4-ounce) frozen wild-caught Alaskan salmon fillets

½ teaspoon kosher salt

1 tablespoon extra-virgin olive oil

5 cubes frozen crushed garlic

1 cup frozen chopped onions

1 cup frozen chopped spinach

⅓ cup chopped sun-dried tomatoes

⅓ cup chopped artichoke hearts

½ cup chicken broth

1 cup heavy cream

2 teaspoons red wine vinegar

½ cup freshly grated Parmesan cheese

2 tablespoons capers

PER SERVING

Calories: 494
Fat: 32g
Protein: 33g
Sodium: 1,058mg

Fiber: 3g
Carbohydrates: 13g
Sugar: 6g

1. Remove fish from wrappers and rinse each piece in cold water for 30 seconds to remove any ice or frost on the surface. Pat dry with paper towels and salt both sides of the fish. (Fish will still be frozen.)

2. Heat a large skillet over medium heat. When hot, add oil and fish with skin-side up. Cook for 4 minutes before flipping skin-side down and cooking until salmon easily flakes with a fork, another 4 minutes. Remove from the skillet.

3. In the same skillet, over high heat, add garlic, onions, spinach, tomatoes, and artichokes. Sauté until onions soften, about 3 minutes. Add broth, cream, vinegar, Parmesan, and capers. Bring to a gentle simmer, then immediately return fish to skillet. Spoon sauce over fillets and cook for another minute. Serve immediately.

SPICY TOMATO CRAB RAVIOLI

This is such a simple recipe, but the taste is simply marvelous. This has a bit of kick from the red pepper flakes—feel free to add more if you prefer. If you are unfamiliar with clam juice, you can often find it by the canned seafood at your grocery store.

SERVES: 4
PREP TIME: 10 minutes
COOK TIME: 17 minutes
TOTAL TIME: 27 minutes

Ingredients

1¾ teaspoons kosher salt, divided

1 (25-ounce) bag frozen cheese ravioli

3 tablespoons salted butter

5 cubes frozen crushed garlic

1 (28-ounce) can crushed tomatoes, undrained

½ cup clam juice

¼ teaspoon red pepper flakes

2 tablespoons red wine vinegar

8 ounces fresh lump crabmeat

½ cup freshly grated Parmesan cheese

PER SERVING

Calories: 577
Fat: 19g
Protein: 30g
Sodium: 1,973mg

Fiber: 6g
Carbohydrates: 70g
Sugar: 12g

1. In a large pot, bring 3 quarts water to a boil. Add 1 teaspoon salt and ravioli. Cook for 4 minutes and drain. Set aside.

2. While ravioli cooks, heat a large skillet over high heat. When hot, add butter and garlic. Sauté for 1 minute, then add tomatoes, clam juice, pepper flakes, vinegar, and remaining ¾ teaspoon salt. Bring to a boil, reduce heat and simmer until sauce thickens, about 10–15 minutes.

3. Add crabmeat and allow it to heat through, about 2 minutes, before adding ravioli. Toss to coat and allow ravioli to reheat before topping with Parmesan. Serve immediately.

GREEK AVOCADO SALMON SALAD

This recipe makes an excellent dinner on a warm night outside on the patio. You can serve this with a loaf of warm, crusty bread on the side and add a few artichoke hearts to the salad for a boost in the Greek flavors.

SERVES: 4
PREP TIME: 10 minutes
COOK TIME: 8 minutes
TOTAL TIME: 18 minutes

Dressing

2 cubes frozen crushed garlic

2 tablespoons lemon juice

1 teaspoon kosher salt

½ teaspoon ground black pepper

2 tablespoons extra-virgin olive oil

Salad

1 pound frozen wild-caught Alaskan salmon fillets

2 medium romaine lettuce hearts, cored and chopped

1 medium cucumber, chopped

2 medium Roma tomatoes, cored and chopped

1 small red onion, peeled and sliced thinly

2 medium avocados, peeled, pitted, and chopped

20 Kalamata olives, roughly chopped

½ cup (2 ounces) crumbled feta cheese

PER SERVING

Calories: 500
Fat: 30g
Protein: 34g
Sodium: 1,177mg

Fiber: 12g
Carbohydrates: 24g
Sugar: 8g

1. To make the dressing, in a small bowl, mash garlic with lemon juice, salt, and pepper. Drizzle in oil while whisking.

2. To make the salad, remove fish from wrappers and rinse each piece in cold water for 30 seconds to remove any ice or frost on the surface. Pat dry with paper towels and rub a small amount of the dressing onto the surface of the salmon, reserving most of the dressing for the salad. (Fish will still be frozen.)

3. Heat a large nonstick skillet over medium heat and grease with nonstick spray. When hot, add salmon, skin-side down, and cook for 4–5 minutes until brown. Flip and cook another 4–5 minutes until fish reaches desired level of doneness. Remove from skillet and use a fork to break into large pieces.

4. In a large bowl, combine lettuce, cucumber, tomatoes, onion, avocado, olives, feta, salmon pieces, and remaining dressing. Toss together and serve immediately.

SEAFOOD FETTUCCINE ALFREDO

A creamy, garlicky sauce surrounds the sautéed scallops, shrimp, and thick pasta noodles in this comfort food classic. Feel free to add some frozen vegetables during the last couple of minutes of cooking the sauce to boost the nutritional value. Peas, broccoli, pearl onions, asparagus, or mushrooms would all complement the finished dish wonderfully.

SERVES: 4
PREP TIME: 10 minutes
COOK TIME: 20 minutes
TOTAL TIME: 30 minutes

Ingredients

1¼ teaspoons kosher salt, divided

8 ounces uncooked fettuccine pasta

½ pound frozen raw peeled and deveined medium shrimp

½ pound frozen raw sea scallops

6 tablespoons salted butter, divided

4 cubes frozen crushed garlic, divided

2 tablespoons lemon juice, divided

¼ teaspoon ground black pepper, divided

4 medium green onions, trimmed and chopped

1 cup chicken broth

2 cups heavy cream

1 cup freshly grated Parmesan cheese

2 medium Roma tomatoes, cored and diced

SEAFOOD FETTUCCINE ALFREDO CONT.

1. In a medium pot, bring 2 quarts water to a boil. Add ¾ teaspoon salt and fettuccine. Cook according to package directions, drain, and set aside.

2. Place frozen shrimp and scallops in a large mesh strainer under cold running water for about 5 minutes to thaw. Move pieces around a few times to assist in the thawing process. Slice scallops in half.

3. Heat a large skillet over high heat. When hot, add 2 tablespoons butter, 1 garlic cube, 1 tablespoon lemon juice, scallops, ¼ teaspoon salt, and ⅛ teaspoon pepper. Sauté until scallops are translucent, about 3–4 minutes. (Do not overcook or they will become rubbery.) Remove from skillet and set aside.

4. Return skillet to high heat. Add 2 tablespoons butter, 1 garlic cube, remaining 1 tablespoon lemon juice, shrimp, remaining ¼ teaspoon salt, and remaining ⅛ teaspoon pepper. Sauté just until shrimp turn pink, about 3–4 minutes. Remove from skillet and set aside.

5. Return skillet to high heat. Add remaining 2 tablespoons butter, remaining 2 garlic cubes, and onions. Sauté for 1 minute before adding broth. Bring to a boil, reduce heat, and simmer for 6 minutes, allowing liquid to reduce significantly. Stir in cream and continue to simmer for 5 minutes longer before adding Parmesan, tomatoes, seafood, and cooked fettuccine. Toss to coat the pasta and serve.

PER SERVING

Calories: 1,056	Fiber: 4g
Fat: 66g	Carbohydrates: 56g
Protein: 44g	Sugar: 6g
Sodium: 2,025mg	

SHRIMP QUESADILLAS

These divine quesadillas have such a light and fresh flavor. The melty cheese holds all the goodness inside together perfectly. Plus, these quesadillas come together in about 15 minutes, which makes them a fabulous option when you are tempted to call for takeout because time is short. You could also top these with a little sour cream or salsa.

SERVES: 4
PREP TIME: 7 minutes
COOK TIME: 8 minutes
TOTAL TIME: 15 minutes

Ingredients

16 frozen fully cooked peeled and deveined medium shrimp

1 medium avocado, peeled, pitted, and diced

½ medium jalapeño pepper, cored, seeded, and minced

1 medium Roma tomato, cored and diced

⅓ cup frozen diced onions

¼ cup chopped fresh cilantro

4 teaspoons lime juice

½ teaspoon kosher salt

¼ teaspoon ground black pepper

1½ cups (6 ounces) shredded Colby jack cheese

8 (6") flour tortillas

1. Preheat a large skillet to medium heat. Place frozen shrimp in a small mesh strainer under cold running water for about 5 minutes to thaw. Remove tails and chop into small pieces.

2. In a medium bowl, place shrimp and add avocado, jalapeño, tomato, onions, cilantro, lime juice, salt, and pepper. Mix well.

3. Spread half the Colby jack onto four tortillas. Top with shrimp filling, remaining cheese, and another tortilla. Cook in the skillet until brown on bottom side, about 4 minutes, then flip and cook the second side for another 4 minutes. Cut into wedges and serve.

PER SERVING

Calories: 444
Fat: 21g
Protein: 23g
Sodium: 1,234mg
Fiber: 4g
Carbohydrates: 38g
Sugar: 3g

PANFRIED SALMON CAKES

These classic panfried fish patties are a Southern favorite. It's important to dice both the salmon and the bread quite small so the cakes can stay together after you form them. These are perfect with just a squeeze of fresh lemon juice over the top, but if you like tartar sauce, use that too.

SERVES: 8
PREP TIME: 18 minutes
COOK TIME: 12 minutes
TOTAL TIME: 30 minutes

Ingredients

1½ pounds frozen wild-caught Alaskan salmon fillets

2 slices hearty white bread, finely diced

¼ cup mayonnaise

2 medium green onions, trimmed and finely diced

1 tablespoon lemon juice

1½ teaspoons kosher salt

1 teaspoon dried parsley

½ cup all-purpose flour

2 large eggs, beaten

2 tablespoons water

1 cup panko bread crumbs

½ cup freshly grated Parmesan cheese

½ teaspoon garlic powder

⅓ cup vegetable oil

1. Remove salmon from packaging. Place in a 9" × 13" baking pan and under cold running water for 15 minutes. (Fish will still be slightly frozen.) Pat fish dry with paper towels, remove skin, and dice into small pieces.

2. While fish is thawing, in a medium bowl, combine bread, mayonnaise, onions, lemon juice, salt, and parsley. Add diced salmon to this mixture and use your hands to combine well. Make eight equal patties, about ½" thick.

3. Place flour in a small bowl. In a separate small bowl, combine eggs with water. In a third small bowl, combine bread crumbs, Parmesan, and garlic.

4. Dredge each salmon patty first in the flour, then the egg mixture, and finally the bread crumb mixture, pressing breading onto all sides. Set on a clean plate.

5. Heat oil in a large skillet over medium-high heat. When hot, add four of the patties and cook until browned, about 3 minutes. Flip and cook for another 3 minutes. Repeat with remaining patties. Serve immediately.

PER SERVING

Calories: 390	Fiber: 1g
Fat: 21g	Carbohydrates: 22g
Protein: 25g	Sugar: 1g
Sodium: 749mg	

CITRUS BASIL COD

Transform frozen cod fillets into a showstopping dinner that is done in 15 minutes! For this recipe, the fish gently braises on the stovetop in a citrus basil sauce, and it comes out perfectly tender and tasting terrific every time. This recipe does create a beautiful pan sauce that could be spooned over some steamed rice or vegetables on the side, so feel free to add those to your menu as well.

SERVES: 6
PREP TIME: 5 minutes
COOK TIME: 10 minutes
TOTAL TIME: 15 minutes

Ingredients

1½ pounds frozen wild-caught Alaskan cod fillets

1 teaspoon kosher salt, divided

½ teaspoon ground black pepper, divided

2 tablespoons salted butter

2 cubes frozen crushed garlic

Juice of 1 medium lemon

Juice of 2 medium oranges

4 cubes frozen chopped basil

2 teaspoons brown sugar

PER SERVING

Calories: 118
Fat: 5g
Protein: 17g
Sodium: 516mg

Fiber: 0g
Carbohydrates: 3g
Sugar: 2g

1. Remove fish from wrappers and rinse each piece in cold water for 30 seconds to remove any ice or frost on the surface. Pat dry with paper towels and sprinkle both sides with ½ teaspoon salt and ¼ teaspoon pepper. (Fish will still be frozen.)

2. Heat a large skillet over medium-high heat. When hot, add butter and garlic. Sauté for 1 minute, then add fish, lemon juice, and orange juice. Cover and simmer for 4 minutes before flipping fish over. Cover and cook until fish easily flakes with a fork, another 3–4 minutes.

3. Use a large spatula to remove fish from skillet. Add basil, brown sugar, remaining ½ teaspoon salt, and remaining ¼ teaspoon pepper to the skillet. Simmer for 1–2 minutes to allow sauce to thicken. Turn off heat and return fish to skillet to serve.

AVOCADO ALMOND TUNA WRAPS

This superfresh wrap is bursting with the fresh flavors of tuna, almonds, avocado, cucumber, peppers, and water chestnuts. Go ahead and try mixing up the recipe with different types of veggies you love. There really isn't a way to go wrong with this wrap. Since the frozen onions and peppers are chopped so small, there is no need to thaw them first. Just toss them into the bowl, and they will thaw in just a few minutes after you mix it all together.

SERVES: 8
PREP TIME: 10 minutes
COOK TIME: N/A
TOTAL TIME: 10 minutes

Ingredients

2 (12-ounce) cans solid white albacore tuna in water, drained

1 small stalk celery, trimmed and diced

½ medium cucumber, diced

1 (8-ounce) can water chestnuts, drained and chopped

½ cup frozen chopped onions

½ cup frozen chopped green bell peppers

½ cup slivered toasted almonds

½ cup mayonnaise

1 tablespoon lemon juice

¾ teaspoon kosher salt

½ teaspoon ground black pepper

2 medium avocados, peeled, pitted, and sliced

8 flatbread wraps

1. In a medium bowl, place tuna; flake with a fork. Add celery, cucumber, water chestnuts, onions, peppers, almonds, mayonnaise, lemon juice, salt, and pepper. Mix well.

2. To assemble each wrap, layer avocado down the center of the flatbread. Top with tuna salad. Roll up and serve.

PER SERVING

Calories: 378
Fat: 21g
Protein: 25g
Sodium: 785mg

Fiber: 14g
Carbohydrates: 31g
Sugar: 2g

BLACKENED LIME MAHI-MAHI

Mahi-mahi is a firm-fleshed fish that has a mild, sweet flavor. You could also substitute frozen cod in this recipe and still have great results. The generous squeeze of lime juice over the finished fillet is really important for this blackened dish. That brightness cuts through the intensity of the spices!

SERVES: 4
PREP TIME: 5 minutes
COOK TIME: 15 minutes
TOTAL TIME: 20 minutes

Ingredients

4 (4-ounce) frozen wild-caught mahi-mahi fillets

2 teaspoons paprika

2 teaspoons dried parsley

1 teaspoon dried oregano

1 teaspoon garlic powder

1 teaspoon chili powder

½ teaspoon kosher salt

½ teaspoon ground black pepper

½ teaspoon cumin

⅛ teaspoon ground cayenne pepper

2 teaspoons vegetable oil

Juice of 1 medium lime

PER SERVING

Calories: 131
Fat: 4g
Protein: 3g
Sodium: 412mg
Fiber: 1g
Carbohydrates: 2g
Sugar: 0g

1. Preheat oven to 450°F. Grease a baking sheet with non-stick spray.

2. Remove fish from wrappers and rinse each piece in cold water for 30 seconds to remove any ice or frost on the surface. Pat dry with paper towels. (Fish will still be frozen.)

3. In a small bowl, mix together paprika, parsley, oregano, garlic powder, chili powder, salt, black pepper, cumin, cayenne pepper, and oil to form a paste. Rub onto the outsides of the fish. It should be a thick coating on both sides.

4. Place fish on prepared baking sheet and bake until fish easily flakes with a fork, about 15–17 minutes, depending on the thickness of your fillets. Squeeze a generous amount of lime juice on top of each fillet as soon as it comes out of the oven, and serve.

Chapter Seven
VEGETARIAN MAIN DISHES

THE #MEATLESSMONDAYS HASHTAG IS POPULAR ON SOCIAL MEDIA WITH GOOD REASON. WORKING NO-MEAT RECIPES INTO YOUR WEEKLY MENU PLAN HAS MANY BENEFITS. FIRST OFF, MEAT IS EXPENSIVE! IF YOU ARE LOOKING TO REDUCE YOUR WEEKLY GROCERY BUDGET, THROW IN A VEGETARIAN RECIPE FOR A DAY OR TWO. VEGETABLES, BEANS, AND MOST GRAINS ARE FRIENDLY ON THE WALLET. SECOND, VEGETABLES ARE KIND TO YOUR BODY AND THE EARTH'S NATURAL RESOURCES.

THE RECIPES IN THIS CHAPTER WILL LEAVE YOU FEELING FULL AND NOT MISSING MEAT AT ALL, THANKS TO THE MOUTHWATERING FLAVOR COMBINATIONS. THE BUTTERNUT SQUASH AND BLACK BEAN PITAS WITH AVOCADO AND CILANTRO LIME CREMA ARE ESPECIALLY DELICIOUS. LET VEGETABLES SHINE WITH THESE DELIGHTFUL DISHES.

MEDITERRANEAN QUESADILLAS

This recipe might sound like a culinary conflict, but I promise you, the two types of cuisine pair perfectly. If you don't like olives, keep this in mind: There are only a few Kalamata olives in the whole recipe, and they're chopped up very finely. Plus, they add that ideal hint of brininess to round out the salty feta cheese. Try them at least once!

SERVES: 4
PREP TIME: 10 minutes
COOK TIME: 4 minutes
TOTAL TIME: 14 minutes

Ingredients

2 cups frozen chopped spinach

1 cup frozen chopped onions

2 cubes frozen crushed garlic

½ cup drained bottled roasted red peppers, chopped

16 Kalamata olives, finely chopped

½ cup quartered artichoke hearts, chopped

2 teaspoons red wine vinegar

½ teaspoon dried oregano

½ teaspoon kosher salt

¼ teaspoon ground black pepper

8 (6") flour tortillas

2½ cups (12 ounces) shredded mozzarella cheese, divided

1 cup (4 ounces) crumbled feta cheese, divided

1. Preheat griddle to medium-high heat.

2. In a medium microwave-safe bowl, microwave spinach and onions on high for 2 minutes. Remove and drain in a mesh strainer lined with a double layer of paper towels. Remove as much liquid as possible by squeezing spinach inside the paper towels. Return to bowl.

3. Add garlic, red peppers, olives, artichokes, vinegar, oregano, salt, and black pepper. Mix well, ensuring garlic is evenly incorporated.

4. To assemble each quesadilla, layer one tortilla with 2–3 tablespoons mozzarella, one-fourth of the vegetable mixture, ¼ cup feta, another 2–3 tablespoons mozzarella, and another tortilla. Repeat for remaining quesadillas. Cook on the griddle until golden brown, about 2 minutes. Flip and brown on the second side, another 2 minutes. Serve immediately.

PER SERVING

Calories: 581	Fiber: 5g
Fat: 27g	Carbohydrates: 48g
Protein: 31g	Sugar: 9g
Sodium: 2,141mg	

LOADED WAFFLE FRY NACHOS

Can you call something nachos if there aren't any tortilla chips involved? I say yes, but only if you replace the chips with crispy waffle fries. This is a meatless dish that your family will rave about, but no one needs to know how simple it was to make! One look at all the fabulous toppings and everyone will think you spent ages making dinner.

SERVES: 4
PREP TIME: 10 minutes
COOK TIME: 20 minutes
TOTAL TIME: 30 minutes

Ingredients

1 (22-ounce) bag frozen waffle fries

2 cups (8 ounces) shredded pepper jack cheese

1 cup refried beans

½ cup frozen corn

2 medium Roma tomatoes, cored and chopped

1 medium avocado, peeled, pitted, and chopped

2 medium green onions, trimmed and chopped

⅓ cup sour cream

¼ cup sliced black olives

¼ cup pickled jalapeños

2 tablespoons chopped fresh cilantro

Juice of ½ medium lime

1. Preheat oven to 450°F. Spread fries on rimmed baking sheet and bake for 15 minutes.

2. Remove from the oven and sprinkle pepper jack over the fries. Dollop beans across the fries, then sprinkle on the corn. Return to the oven for another 5 minutes.

3. Remove and top with tomatoes, avocado, onions, sour cream, olives, jalapeños, cilantro, and lime juice. Serve immediately.

PER SERVING

Calories: 629	Fiber: 9g
Fat: 34g	Carbohydrates: 55g
Protein: 22g	Sugar: 3g
Sodium: 1,270mg	

CHEESY ITALIAN ZUCCHINI AND SPINACH BAKE

This dish is not only yummy; it's low-carb as well. It's almost like lasagna, but is healthier and cooks in a fraction of the time! Since both the frozen zucchini and frozen spinach have a high water content, be sure to use the paper towel tricks (as instructed) to keep your dish from ending up soupy. A note: True Parmesan cheese includes rennet, which is an animal-based enzyme. You can find vegetarian "Parmesan" at the store now, but traditional Parmesan won't be vegetarian due to the rennet.

SERVES: 6
PREP TIME: 12 minutes
COOK TIME: 18 minutes
TOTAL TIME: 30 minutes

Ingredients

1 (16-ounce) bag frozen grilled zucchini strips

1 (10-ounce) bag frozen chopped spinach

4 cubes frozen crushed garlic

4 cubes frozen chopped basil

1 (15-ounce) container ricotta cheese

2 cups (8 ounces) shredded mozzarella cheese, divided

¼ cup freshly grated vegetarian Parmesan cheese

1 large egg

1 teaspoon kosher salt

½ teaspoon ground black pepper

1½ cups prepared marinara sauce, divided

PER SERVING

Calories: 332	Fiber: 4g
Fat: 18g	Carbohydrates: 16g
Protein: 23g	Sugar: 6g
Sodium: 1,120mg	

1. Preheat oven to 450°F. Grease a 7" × 11" pan with non-stick spray.

2. Place a single layer of zucchini strips on two microwave-safe plates lined with a double layer of paper towels. Microwave on high for 2 minutes each. Use additional paper towels to press down on the zucchini to remove excess moisture. Set aside.

3. Microwave bag of spinach on high for 2 minutes. Remove and drain spinach in a mesh strainer lined with a double layer of paper towels. Remove as much water as possible by squeezing spinach inside the paper towels until it stops dripping. Set aside.

4. While zucchini and spinach are heating, in a medium bowl, use a rubber spatula to mash together the cubes of garlic and basil. Add ricotta, 1 cup mozzarella, Parmesan, egg, salt, pepper, and spinach. Mix together well.

5. Spread ¾ cup marinara sauce in prepared pan, then spread half of the zucchini strips to cover bottom of the pan. Spread cheese mixture on top, then evenly layer the second half of the zucchini on top of the cheese. Spread on remaining ¾ cup marinara sauce, then sprinkle remaining 1 cup mozzarella over the top. Bake until hot and bubbly on the edges, about 18 minutes. Serve immediately.

CHEESY VEGETABLE SOUP

If you are working to introduce more veggies into your diet, this soup is a great way to do it. This recipe goes great with a hot loaf of crusty bread on the side for dipping in the broth. If you want to add one more vegetable, toss in some frozen peas.

SERVES: 8
PREP TIME: 10 minutes
COOK TIME: 16 minutes
TOTAL TIME: 26 minutes

Ingredients

4 tablespoons salted butter

4 cubes frozen crushed garlic

1½ cups frozen chopped onions

¾ cup frozen sliced carrots

¾ cup frozen sliced white mushrooms

2 medium stalks celery, trimmed and chopped

¾ cup all-purpose flour

6 cups vegetable broth

1 cup half and half

2 cups (8 ounces) shredded sharp Cheddar cheese

1 (12-ounce) bag frozen broccoli florets

1 (12-ounce) bag frozen cauliflower

1 teaspoon kosher salt

1 teaspoon ground black pepper

1. Heat a large pot over high heat. When hot, add butter, garlic, onions, carrots, mushrooms, and celery. Sauté until vegetables soften, about 3–4 minutes. Add flour and stir. Reduce heat to medium-high and cook for 1 minute before adding broth. Continue to stir and allow the mixture to come to a boil and thicken, about 5 minutes.

2. Add half and half and Cheddar. Stir and allow Cheddar to melt and combine with broth before adding broccoli, cauliflower, salt, and pepper, about 2 minutes. Bring to a gentle boil, reduce heat, and simmer for 5 minutes before serving.

PER SERVING

Calories: 298
Fat: 17g
Protein: 12g
Sodium: 1,185mg

Fiber: 4g
Carbohydrates: 20g
Sugar: 6g

CARAMELIZED ONION AND PEAR GRILLED CHEESE SANDWICHES

These simple sandwiches are a new twist on the classic grilled cheese. The distinctive combination of sweet, savory, salty, and tangy comes together between two gorgeous pieces of grilled sourdough bread. If you decide to play with the cheeses, stick to keeping one mild and melty, and let the other be more pungent and stronger. You need the balance of both in this special sandwich. The recipe calls for red pears, but any type of pear would work well.

SERVES: 4
PREP TIME: 5 minutes
COOK TIME: 13 minutes
TOTAL TIME: 18 minutes

Ingredients

6 tablespoons salted butter, softened, divided

2 cups frozen chopped onions

½ teaspoon kosher salt

4 (1-ounce) slices Swiss cheese

8 slices hearty sourdough bread

4 ounces Brie cheese, thinly sliced

2 medium-sized firm but ripe red pears, cored and thinly sliced

PER SERVING

Calories: 618	Fiber: 5g
Fat: 33g	Carbohydrates: 55g
Protein: 21g	Sugar: 16g
Sodium: 980mg	

1. Heat a large skillet over high heat. When hot, add 2 tablespoons butter, onions, and salt. Sauté on high until extra moisture evaporates, about 2 minutes, then reduce heat to medium-high and cook onions until dark brown in color, about 5 minutes. Remove from skillet and set aside.

2. Assemble each sandwich with 1 slice of Swiss on one piece of bread and 1 ounce Brie on the other. Add ½ of a sliced pear and top with one-fourth of the onions. Top sandwich with another piece of bread, and butter outsides of sandwiches with 1 tablespoon butter on each slice.

3. Return skillet to medium heat. When hot, add sandwiches. Cook until golden brown, about 3 minutes per side. Serve immediately.

SPINACH AND ARTICHOKE–STUFFED PORTOBELLO MUSHROOMS

Portobello mushrooms are the vegetarian equivalent of a thick, juicy steak, and here, they're stuffed with a creamy combo of spinach and artichokes. *This is how you convert someone to try out Meatless Mondays. Plus, they are simply gorgeous when you pull them from the oven! When it's time to clean the mushrooms, the key is to wipe them with a damp towel. (If you rinse them with water, they will absorb it and turn slimy.)*

SERVES: 4
PREP TIME: 10 minutes
COOK TIME: 20 minutes
TOTAL TIME: 30 minutes

Ingredients

4 large (4"-diameter) portobello mushroom caps

3 tablespoons extra-virgin olive oil, divided

3 cubes frozen crushed garlic, divided

¾ teaspoon kosher salt

¼ teaspoon ground black pepper

1 (10-ounce) bag frozen spinach

4 ounces cream cheese, softened

3 tablespoons mayonnaise

½ cup freshly grated Parmesan cheese, divided

¾ teaspoon dried thyme, divided

1 (14-ounce) can artichoke hearts, drained and chopped

½ cup panko bread crumbs

PER SERVING

Calories: 423
Fat: 29g
Protein: 12g
Sodium: 1,128mg

Fiber: 5g
Carbohydrates: 24g
Sugar: 5g

1. Preheat oven to 450°F. Lightly grease a baking sheet with nonstick spray.

2. Use a spoon to scrape the gills from the insides of mushroom caps. Set mushrooms on the prepared baking sheet, bottom-side up.

3. In a small bowl, combine 2 tablespoons oil and 2 garlic cubes. Brush insides of each mushroom cap with the garlic oil, then sprinkle salt and pepper evenly on each. Bake for 10 minutes.

4. Microwave bag of spinach on high for 2 minutes. Remove and drain spinach in mesh strainer lined with a double layer of paper towels. Remove as much water as possible by squeezing spinach inside the paper towels until it stops dripping.

5. In a medium bowl, combine spinach, cream cheese, mayonnaise, ¼ cup Parmesan, ½ teaspoon thyme, artichokes, and remaining garlic cube. Remove any moisture that has formed in the bottom of the cooked mushroom caps, then fill evenly with the spinach mixture.

6. In a small bowl, mix together remaining 1 tablespoon oil, bread crumbs, remaining ¼ cup Parmesan, and remaining ¼ teaspoon thyme. Sprinkle mixture over the top of each stuffed mushroom. Bake for 10 minutes and serve immediately.

TEX-MEX RICE AND BEANS SKILLET

Loaded with vegetables and spices, this vegetarian dish isn't lacking for anything. Together, the whole-grain brown rice and black beans create a complete protein that your body needs when you aren't eating meat. If you have some on hand, the addition of fresh avocado and cilantro are terrific options to deepen that Tex-Mex experience.

SERVES: 4
PREP TIME: 5 minutes
COOK TIME: 10 minutes
TOTAL TIME: 15 minutes

Ingredients

2 (10-ounce) bags frozen brown rice

1 tablespoon salted butter

3 cubes frozen crushed garlic

1 cup frozen chopped onions

1 cup frozen chopped green bell peppers

1½ teaspoons kosher salt, divided

1 tablespoon chili powder

1 tablespoon cumin

1 tablespoon smoked paprika

1 (10-ounce) can diced tomatoes with green chilies, drained

1 (15-ounce) can black beans, drained and rinsed

1 cup frozen corn

Juice of 1 medium lime

1. Heat rice in microwave according to package directions. Set aside.

2. Heat a large skillet over high heat. When hot, add butter, garlic, onions, peppers, and ½ teaspoon salt. Sauté until vegetables soften, about 3–4 minutes.

3. Add chili powder, cumin, and paprika. Stir and cook for 1 minute before adding tomatoes, beans, and corn. Cook for 3 minutes.

4. Add the rice and remaining 1 teaspoon salt. Stir well and coat the rice with the seasonings. Allow rice to heat through, about 2 minutes, then add lime juice. Mix together before serving.

PER SERVING

Calories: 455

Fat: 5g

Protein: 15g

Sodium: 1,445mg

Fiber: 13g

Carbohydrates: 89g

Sugar: 6g

VEGETARIAN PANINIS

Paninis don't need meat to be hearty and filling. You just need the right combination of vegetables, gooey cheese, and seasonings. If you don't have a panini press to create that distinctive crunch on the outside, you can use an electric skillet and cook one side at a time. Be sure you use something to weigh down the paninis as they cook. That compression is important for the finished product! Try placing a heavy frying pan on top.

SERVES: 8
PREP TIME: 5 minutes
COOK TIME: 9 minutes
TOTAL TIME: 14 minutes

Ingredients

1 tablespoon salted butter

1 cup frozen chopped onions

1 cup frozen sliced white mushrooms

½ teaspoon kosher salt

¼ teaspoon ground black pepper

1 cup frozen chopped spinach

1 loaf (about 8 ounces) baguette-style French bread

½ cup prepared olive tapenade

8 (1-ounce) slices provolone cheese, cut in half

2 medium Roma tomatoes, cored and sliced

½ cup drained bottled roasted red peppers

PER SERVING

Calories: 250	Fiber: 3g
Fat: 13g	Carbohydrates: 20g
Protein: 12g	Sugar: 4g
Sodium: 798mg	

1. Preheat panini press to high.

2. Heat a large skillet over high heat. When hot, add butter, onions, mushrooms, salt, and black pepper. Sauté until vegetables soften, about 3–4 minutes. Add spinach and continue to cook until excess moisture has evaporated, about 3 more minutes. Set aside.

3. Slice baguette on the diagonal into sixteen even slices. Spread each piece with ½ tablespoon tapenade. For each panini, layer one piece of bread with a half slice provolone, then evenly divide tomatoes, red peppers, and sautéed vegetables on top. Top with another half slice provolone and another slice of bread.

4. Grill in panini press until golden brown, about 3–4 minutes. Serve immediately.

BUTTERNUT SQUASH AND BLACK BEAN PITAS WITH AVOCADO AND CILANTRO LIME CREMA

Take your meatless meals south of the border with these unique pitas. A layer of sweet butternut squash gets topped with hearty black beans, avocado, and some salty queso fresco. The finishing touch of the cilantro lime crema crowns this dish with a refreshing cool tanginess.

SERVES: 4
PREP TIME: 10 minutes
COOK TIME: 5 minutes
TOTAL TIME: 15 minutes

Cilantro Lime Crema

½ cup sour cream

4 teaspoons chopped fresh cilantro

Juice of ½ medium lime

1 medium jalapeño pepper, cored, seeded, and finely minced

½ teaspoon kosher salt

⅛ teaspoon ground black pepper

Pitas

1 (10-ounce) bag frozen chopped butternut squash

2 cubes frozen crushed garlic

1 tablespoon salted butter

½ teaspoon chili powder

¼ teaspoon kosher salt

⅛ teaspoon ground black pepper

1 (15-ounce) can black beans, drained and rinsed

4 (6") pitas

¼ cup (1 ounce) crumbled queso fresco

2 medium avocados, peeled, pitted, and sliced

1. To make the crema, in a small bowl, combine sour cream, cilantro, lime juice, jalapeño, salt, and black pepper. Set aside.

2. To make the pitas, cook squash according to package directions, then add to a large bowl. Stir in the garlic, butter, chili powder, salt, and pepper. Mash together with a fork. Set aside.

3. In a small microwave-safe bowl, microwave beans on high until hot, about 1 minute.

4. Warm pitas in the microwave, about 15 seconds each, then evenly divide the squash, beans, queso fresco, and avocados across the tops of each. Top with the cilantro lime crema and serve immediately.

PER SERVING

Calories: 525
Fat: 19g
Protein: 16g
Sodium: 1,117mg

Fiber: 14g
Carbohydrates: 69g
Sugar: 4g

VEGETARIAN THAI NOODLES WITH SPICY PEANUT SAUCE

Thai food provides a distinctive balance among sweet, sour, spicy, and salty ingredients, and these noodles are smothered in a sauce that highlights all four. Don't let the word *spicy* intimidate you; this recipe features a subtle heat. If you want more heat in your noodles, add ¼ teaspoon of red pepper flakes to the sauce.

SERVES: 4
PREP TIME: 10 minutes
COOK TIME: 10 minutes
TOTAL TIME: 20 minutes

Ingredients

3 (3-ounce) packages ramen noodles, seasoning discarded

2 (12-ounce) bags frozen broccoli florets

3 tablespoons sesame oil

3 cubes frozen crushed garlic

3 cubes frozen crushed ginger

¼ cup soy sauce

⅓ cup peanut butter

¼ cup Thai sweet chili sauce

Juice of 1 medium lime

¼ cup water

1 medium red bell pepper, cored, seeded, and thinly sliced

4 medium green onions, trimmed and chopped

¼ cup chopped fresh cilantro

½ cup chopped peanuts

1. In a medium pot, over high heat, bring 7 cups water to a boil. Add ramen and cook for 3 minutes. Drain and set aside.

2. Cook broccoli in microwave according to package directions. Set aside.

3. In a large skillet over medium-low heat, add oil, garlic, and ginger. Keep heat low and sauté for 1 minute before adding soy sauce, peanut butter, chili sauce, lime juice, and water. Stir and allow sauce to heat through, about 2 minutes.

4. Add bell pepper, onions, cilantro, broccoli, and noodles to the sauce and toss to coat. Top with peanuts and serve immediately.

PER SERVING

Calories: 599
Fat: 32g
Protein: 18g
Sodium: 1,412mg

Fiber: 9g
Carbohydrates: 60g
Sugar: 33g

VEGETARIAN COCONUT CURRY WITH RICE

This is a classic Indian curry that uses sweet potatoes and kale instead of the standard proteins. The coconut milk adds a beautiful sweetness that balances out the warm curry powder in the sauce. The kale becomes nice and tender when mixed with the warm ingredients. Including some toasted almonds or pumpkin seeds to the top of each bowl would be great for some added crunch in each bite.

SERVES: 6
PREP TIME: 5 minutes
COOK TIME: 21 minutes
TOTAL TIME: 26 minutes

Ingredients

2 tablespoons salted butter

1 cup frozen chopped onions

5 cubes frozen crushed garlic

3 cubes frozen crushed ginger

2 (10-ounce) bags frozen chopped sweet potatoes

1 (12-ounce) bag frozen chopped kale

1½ teaspoons kosher salt

½ teaspoon ground black pepper

1 cup vegetable broth

1 (14-ounce) can coconut milk

1 teaspoon curry powder

Juice of ½ medium lime

2 (18-ounce) boxes frozen sticky white rice

1. Heat a large pot over high heat. When hot, add butter, onions, garlic, and ginger. Sauté for 3 minutes, then add sweet potatoes, kale, salt, and pepper. Cook for 3 minutes. Add broth, reduce to medium heat, cover, and simmer for 10 minutes.

2. Add coconut milk and curry. Simmer for another 5 minutes before adding lime juice.

3. While curry is cooking, heat rice according to package directions. Serve in bowls with rice first and topped with the curry.

PER SERVING

Calories: 499
Fat: 12g
Protein: 9g
Sodium: 824mg

Fiber: 3g
Carbohydrates: 84g
Sugar: 1g

FETA AND VEGETABLE FRITTATA

A frittata isn't just for breakfast—it also makes a tasty and substantial dinner choice! Sautéed mushrooms, onions, and peppers create the foundation of flavor in this dish, while the feta cheese provides a salty tang to cut through the richness of the eggs. The finishing touch of this frittata comes from a couple of minutes under the broiler to allow the top to caramelize and turn golden brown. If you don't have a 12" oven-safe skillet, you can use a smaller one, but it will need a longer time in the oven.

SERVES: 6
PREP TIME: 5 minutes
COOK TIME: 20 minutes
TOTAL TIME: 25 minutes

Ingredients

8 large eggs

⅓ cup 1% milk

¾ teaspoon kosher salt, divided

¼ teaspoon ground black pepper

¾ cup (3 ounces) crumbled feta cheese

⅓ cup (about 1⅓ ounces) shredded Cheddar cheese

2 tablespoons salted butter

½ cup frozen chopped onions

½ cup frozen chopped green bell peppers

½ cup frozen sliced white mushrooms

½ cup frozen chopped spinach

1. Preheat oven to 350°F.

2. In a medium bowl, whisk together eggs, milk, ½ teaspoon salt, and black pepper. Mix in feta and Cheddar. Set aside.

3. Heat a 12" oven-safe skillet over high heat. When hot, add butter, onions, green peppers, mushrooms, spinach, and remaining ¼ teaspoon salt. Sauté until vegetables soften, about 3–4 minutes. Reduce heat to medium and add egg mixture. Do not stir.

4. Once the eggs have set along the outside edge of the skillet, about 2 minutes, transfer the skillet to the oven and bake for 12 minutes. Turn on the broiler and broil on high for 2 minutes until golden brown. Serve immediately.

PER SERVING

Calories: 222
Fat: 15g
Protein: 14g
Sodium: 646mg

Fiber: 1g
Carbohydrates: 4g
Sugar: 3g

MEATLESS BLACK BEAN CHILI

When a chili tastes as impressive as this one, there is no need for meat! If you want to add some crunch, crumble a few corn tortilla chips on the top of each bowl. A few chunks of fresh avocado are another great topping option.

SERVES: 4
PREP TIME: 5 minutes
COOK TIME: 15 minutes
TOTAL TIME: 20 minutes

Ingredients

1 tablespoon salted butter

1½ cups frozen chopped onions

3 cubes frozen crushed garlic

1 cup frozen chopped green bell peppers

1 teaspoon kosher salt

1 (10-ounce) bag frozen chopped butternut squash

1½ teaspoons chili powder

½ teaspoon cumin

¼ teaspoon cinnamon

1 cup vegetable broth

1 (10-ounce) can diced tomatoes with chilies, undrained

1 (15-ounce) can black beans, drained and rinsed

¼ cup sour cream

1. Heat a large pot over high heat. When hot, add butter, onions, garlic, bell peppers, and salt. Sauté until vegetables soften, about 3–4 minutes. Add squash and continue to cook for another 2 minutes.

2. Add chili powder, cumin, cinnamon, broth, tomatoes with juices, and beans. Bring to a boil, then reduce heat and let simmer for 5 minutes. Serve with a dollop of sour cream in each bowl.

PER SERVING

Calories: 241
Fat: 6g
Protein: 9g
Sodium: 1,323mg

Fiber: 10g
Carbohydrates: 38g
Sugar: 8g

ROASTED VEGETABLE TACOS

Roasting vegetables creates so much flavor because the outside of the vegetables caramelizes thanks to that high heat. You could add some black beans to the tacos and top with queso fresco and cilantro for an even better bite.

SERVES: 10
PREP TIME: 10 minutes
COOK TIME: 20 minutes
TOTAL TIME: 30 minutes

Ingredients

1 (10-ounce) bag frozen chopped sweet potatoes

1 (12-ounce) bag frozen cauliflower florets

2 tablespoons vegetable oil

2 tablespoons plus 1 teaspoon lime juice, divided

1¾ teaspoons kosher salt, divided

1 teaspoon cumin

1 teaspoon paprika

1 teaspoon chili powder

1 teaspoon garlic powder

1 medium avocado, peeled and pitted

¼ cup sour cream

10 corn tortillas

1. Preheat oven to 450°F. Grease a rimmed baking sheet with nonstick spray.

2. In a medium bowl, combine sweet potatoes, cauliflower, oil, 2 tablespoons lime juice, 1 teaspoon salt, cumin, paprika, chili powder, and garlic powder. Toss to evenly coat all vegetables in the seasonings. Spread on prepared baking sheet and roast for 20 minutes.

3. While vegetables roast, mash together avocado, sour cream, remaining 1 teaspoon lime juice, and remaining ¾ teaspoon salt in a small bowl. Set aside.

4. Char tortillas on the open flame of a gas stove. Assemble tacos with vegetable filling and top with avocado mixture. Serve immediately.

PER SERVING

Calories: 149
Fat: 6g
Protein: 3g
Sodium: 439mg

Fiber: 4g
Carbohydrates: 21g
Sugar: 1g

Chapter Eight
DESSERT RECIPES

FOR ANYONE WITH A SWEET TOOTH, DESSERT AT THE END OF A MEAL IS A CELEBRATION UNTO ITSELF. YOU PROBABLY ASSOCIATE HOMEMADE DESSERTS WITH OPTIONS LIKE BROWNIES, CAKES, AND COOKIES MADE FROM ROOM-TEMPERATURE INGREDIENTS—BUT YOU CAN ALSO USE YOUR FREEZER TO CREATE DECADENT TREATS! SURE, WE'LL USE ICE CREAM SOMETIMES, BUT YOU'LL ALSO FIND SOME SURPRISING OPTIONS, INCLUDING DEEP-FRIED CHOCOLATE-COVERED MINI ÉCLAIRS, GRILLED STRAWBERRY CHEESECAKE SANDWICHES, AND DUTCH APPLE PIE BITES. BEST OF ALL, YOU CAN MAKE ALL OF THESE DESSERTS FROM INGREDIENTS IN YOUR FREEZER IN 30 MINUTES OR LESS.

BROWNIE CRUNCH ICE CREAM MIXERS

You don't need an expensive ice cream store to mix additional toppings into a frozen treat—do it at home! All you need is a stand mixer to take on that hard ice cream straight from the freezer. If you don't have a stand mixer, you can still make these treats, but will need a bit more time to let the ice cream soften before you are able to stir in the brownie crunch.

SERVES: 4
PREP TIME: 10 minutes
COOK TIME: N/A
TOTAL TIME: 10 minutes

Ingredients

3 tablespoons salted butter, melted

2 cups boxed brownie mix (about ½ a box)

1 quart vanilla ice cream

¼ cup chocolate syrup

PER SERVING

Calories: 746	Fiber: 1g
Fat: 34g	Carbohydrates: 102g
Protein: 9g	Sugar: 35g
Sodium: 470mg	

1. In a medium bowl, combine melted butter and brownie mix. Stir together until the mixture resembles pea-sized crumbs.

2. Spread mixture onto a large microwave-safe plate and microwave on high for four 1-minute increments, stirring the mixture well between each increment. Place plate in the freezer to cool for 10 minutes.

3. In the bowl of your stand mixer fitted with the paddle attachment, add ice cream straight from the freezer and most of the cooled brownie pieces. Mix just enough to soften ice cream and mix in brownie crumble, just a minute or two. If you mix it too long, it will become too soft.

4. Divide ice cream evenly among four dishes and top with remaining brownie crumble and chocolate syrup. Serve immediately.

LEMON RASPBERRY CHEESECAKE TARTLETS

These individual tartlets are ideal for your next dinner party. Frozen puff pastry shells create a showstopping vessel for the raspberry cream cheese and lemon curd filling. Feel free to swap out the raspberries for other frozen fruits, such as peaches, mango, strawberries, blueberries, or blackberries. If you're feeling extra fancy, melt some chocolate and drizzle it over the top of each tartlet. You can find prepared lemon curd at the grocery store, usually either in the baking aisle or with the jams and jellies.

SERVES: 6
PREP TIME: 14 minutes
COOK TIME: 16 minutes
TOTAL TIME: 30 minutes

Ingredients

1 (10-ounce) box frozen puff pastry shells

6 ounces cream cheese, softened

$\frac{1}{3}$ cup plus 1 tablespoon confectioners' sugar, divided

$\frac{3}{4}$ teaspoon vanilla extract

$\frac{1}{8}$ teaspoon kosher salt

$\frac{1}{3}$ cup frozen raspberries

$\frac{3}{4}$ cup prepared lemon curd

PER SERVING

Calories: 549
Fat: 29g
Protein: 5g
Sodium: 281mg
Fiber: 1g
Carbohydrates: 63g
Sugar: 44g

1. Preheat oven to 425°F.

2. Separate puff pastry shells and place on an ungreased cookie sheet. Bake on the middle rack until golden brown, 16–18 minutes. Transfer to a plate and put in the freezer to cool for a few minutes.

3. While shells bake, in a medium bowl, combine cream cheese, $\frac{1}{3}$ cup confectioners' sugar, vanilla, and salt. Stir until smooth.

4. In a small microwave-safe bowl, heat raspberries at 20 percent power for 20 second increments until thawed. Add the thawed berries to the cream cheese mixture, leaving behind any liquid in the bowl. Mix well.

5. To assemble each tartlet, remove center "hat" of the pastry shell and layer first with the raspberry and cream cheese mixture, then the lemon curd. Finish by sifting remaining 1 tablespoon confectioners' sugar through a fine-mesh strainer over the tops of the tartlets. Serve immediately.

GRILLED STRAWBERRY CHEESECAKE SANDWICHES

The foundation of this scrumptious dessert is grilled slices of frozen pound cake, which beats boring ol' strawberry shortcake any day! Grilling the cream cheese–stuffed sandwich creates a deliciously salty caramelized crust, so don't skip that significant step. You could mix up the flavor profile by using some raspberries, peaches, or blackberries instead of strawberries. To vary the filling, try adding your favorite citrus zest, fresh mint, or almond extract.

SERVES: 6
PREP TIME: 20 minutes
COOK TIME: 4 minutes
TOTAL TIME: 24 minutes

Ingredients

1 pound strawberries, stemmed and sliced

¼ cup granulated sugar

1 (16-ounce) frozen pound cake

1 (8-ounce) container whipped cream cheese

2 tablespoons confectioners' sugar

½ teaspoon vanilla extract

2 tablespoons salted butter

PER SERVING

Calories: 452
Fat: 19g
Protein: 6g
Sodium: 461mg

Fiber: 2g
Carbohydrates: 61g
Sugar: 41g

1. Preheat griddle to medium heat.

2. In a medium bowl, mix together strawberries with granulated sugar. Set aside for 15 minutes and let syrup form.

3. Use a serrated knife to cut frozen pound cake into twelve slices. Spread them out to begin thawing.

4. In a small bowl, mix together cream cheese, confectioners' sugar, and vanilla. Set aside.

5. Butter one side of each piece of cake. Turn six cake slices over and spread on the cream cheese mixture. Top with the remaining six pieces of buttered cake, being sure buttered sides are all facing out.

6. Grill each sandwich until golden brown, about 2 minutes a side. Plate and top with strawberries and syrup. Serve immediately.

DEEP-FRIED CHOCOLATE-COVERED MINI ÉCLAIRS

If you love deep-fried treats at your local fair, you will be obsessed with these indulgent gems. Each frozen éclair is coated in a light batter, then fried until the chocolate on the outside of the pastry melts, but the interior cream is still cold. It makes for perfect bites of both taste and temperature.

SERVES: 30
PREP TIME: 5 minutes
COOK TIME: 24 minutes
TOTAL TIME: 29 minutes

Ingredients

1 (48-ounce) bottle frying oil

1 large egg

¾ cup plus 2 tablespoons 1% milk

1¼ cups all-purpose flour

1 teaspoon baking powder

¼ teaspoon kosher salt

1 (14-ounce) container frozen chocolate-covered mini éclairs

2 tablespoons confectioners' sugar

PER SERVING

Calories: 75
Fat: 5g
Protein: 1g
Sodium: 39mg

Fiber: 0g
Carbohydrates: 7g
Sugar: 3g

1. Pour frying oil into a deep fryer or large pot to a depth of at least 3". Heat oil to 365°F.

2. In a medium bowl, whisk together egg, milk, flour, baking powder, and salt. Spear frozen éclair with two forks and twist around to coat it completely with the batter.

3. Put five éclairs into the oil and fry until golden brown, about 2 minutes. Flip to brown on the second side, about 2 minutes. Repeat with remaining éclairs and dust with confectioners' sugar. Serve hot.

PEACH PIE ROLL-UPS

You may never make a "normal" fruit pie after making these lemon-glazed, bite-sized peach pies. They are very easy to prepare—you can even teach the little ones in your family how to do it. Serve hot from the oven with a nice scoop of vanilla ice cream.

SERVES: 12
PREP TIME: 10 minutes
COOK TIME: 18 minutes
TOTAL TIME: 28 minutes

Ingredients

⅓ cup granulated sugar

¼ teaspoon ground nutmeg

1 teaspoon cinnamon

1 (9") refrigerated piecrust

2 tablespoons salted butter, melted, divided

12 slices frozen peaches

¾ cup confectioners' sugar

2 teaspoons lemon juice

PER SERVING

Calories: 161
Fat: 6g
Protein: 1g
Sodium: 94mg

Fiber: 1g
Carbohydrates: 25g
Sugar: 15g

1. Preheat oven to 425°F. Line a baking sheet with parchment paper.

2. In a small bowl, combine granulated sugar, nutmeg, and cinnamon. Set aside.

3. Unroll piecrust on cutting board and brush entire surface with about 1 tablespoon melted butter. Cover with sugar mixture, saving about 1 tablespoon to sprinkle over the tops after rolling them up.

4. Cut circle of dough into twelve equal triangular slices. For each roll-up, place 1 frozen peach slice on the wide end of a dough triangle and roll toward the narrow end (no need to seal the ends). Place on baking sheet. Repeat.

5. Brush remaining 1 tablespoon melted butter over tops of finished rolls and sprinkle on rest of cinnamon sugar. Bake on middle rack until golden brown, 18–20 minutes.

6. Combine confectioners' sugar and lemon juice to form a glaze. Remove rolls from oven and drizzle glaze over the top of each roll-up. Serve warm.

MINT BROWNIE WAFFLE SUNDAES

Yes, you can make brownies in your waffle iron! All you need is your favorite brownie mix and one extra egg for warm brownies in a matter of minutes. If mint isn't your favorite, you could substitute peanut butter chips and peanut butter ice cream. Or what about butterscotch chips and butter pecan ice cream? You can't go wrong with plain chocolate chips and vanilla ice cream either!

SERVES: 8
PREP TIME: 5 minutes
COOK TIME: 15 minutes
TOTAL TIME: 20 minutes

Ingredients

1 (18-ounce) box brownie mix

Eggs, oil, and water as directed on brownie mix box

1 additional large egg

1 cup Andes mint chocolate baking chips

4 cups mint chocolate chip ice cream

1 cup prepared hot fudge sauce

PER SERVING

Calories: 866
Fat: 44g
Protein: 10g
Sodium: 409mg

Fiber: 2g
Carbohydrates: 107g
Sugar: 44g

1. Preheat waffle iron. Lightly grease with nonstick spray.

2. In a medium bowl, prepare brownie mix with the directed amounts of eggs, oil, and water from the box. Add the additional egg and baking chips. Mix well.

3. Completely fill hot waffle iron with batter (depending on your waffle iron size, it might make 2 or more waffles). Cook until done based on waffle iron instructions. Use two forks to pull waffles out of the iron. If waffles are too soft, turn iron over to remove them.

4. Heat hot fudge according to jar directions.

5. Cut waffles into triangles and divide among bowls. Top each warm waffle triangle with ½ cup ice cream and 2 tablespoons hot fudge. Serve immediately.

FROSTED CIRCUS ANIMAL COOKIE ICE CREAM CAKE

A foundation of strawberry shortcake ice cream bars gets layered with a frosted animal cookie crumble and ice cream for a supereasy dessert that you will make over and over again. You can create your own version of this cake by switching out the vanilla ice cream for a different flavor. A berry sherbet would work well, or if you want a more intense fruit flavor, go for a strawberry or raspberry sorbet instead.

SERVES: 8
PREP TIME: 15 minutes
COOK TIME: N/A
TOTAL TIME: 15 minutes

Ingredients

1 pint vanilla ice cream

1 (12-ounce) bag frosted circus animal cookies, divided

3 ounces cream cheese

8 strawberry shortcake ice cream bars

2 tablespoons rainbow nonpareil sprinkles

PER SERVING

Calories: 480
Fat: 25g
Protein: 4g
Sodium: 244mg

Fiber: 1g
Carbohydrates: 60g
Sugar: 38g

1. Remove ice cream from freezer to soften.

2. Set aside 20 cookies and put the rest in the bowl of a food processor. Pulse until they form uniform crumbs. Add cream cheese and pulse to incorporate. Set aside.

3. Slide sticks out of ice cream bars and discard. Layer 6 ice cream bars in the bottom of a 7" × 11" baking pan. Cut the last 2 bars into slices and fill in the gaps in the baking pan. Top with cookie crumbles and press down firmly to compact the cookie crumble layer.

4. Spread shallow scoops of ice cream on top of the bars. Roughly chop remaining 20 cookies with a knife and spread over ice cream, along with the sprinkles. Serve immediately or cover before storing in the freezer for up to 2 weeks.

PEACH DESSERT PIZZA

Dessert pizza is a fun way to finish any meal. This recipe uses frozen Toaster Strudels for a quick and easy foundation. If peaches aren't your thing, you can simply substitute some fresh apples or frozen blueberries.

SERVES: 8
PREP TIME: 5 minutes
COOK TIME: 21 minutes
TOTAL TIME: 26 minutes

Ingredients

8 frozen Pillsbury Cinnamon Roll Toaster Strudels

1 (1-pound) bag frozen peaches

¼ cup water

½ cup brown sugar

¾ teaspoon cinnamon

¾ teaspoon ground nutmeg

1 tablespoon lemon juice

⅓ cup all-purpose flour

⅓ cup confectioners' sugar

2½ tablespoons salted butter

PER SERVING

Calories: 354	Fiber: 2g
Fat: 11g	Carbohydrates: 64g
Protein: 3g	Sugar: 48g
Sodium: 225mg	

1. Preheat oven to 400°F. Grease a 9" × 13" baking pan with nonstick spray.

2. Remove strudels from packaging; set aside frosting packets. Arrange strudels on prepared pan. Bake on the middle rack for 5 minutes. Set aside, but leave strudels on the pan.

3. While strudels bake, heat a large nonstick skillet over medium-high heat. When hot, add peaches and water. Cover and cook for 3 minutes. Add brown sugar, cinnamon, nutmeg, and lemon juice. Stir and continue to cook until peaches are soft and sauce thickens, about 5 minutes. Use a wooden spoon to cut peach slices in half.

4. In a medium bowl, combine flour and confectioners' sugar. Using a pastry cutter or two forks, cut butter into dry ingredients until mixture is the size of small peas.

5. Spread peaches over each strudel. Squeeze handfuls of the crumble to compact, then break into smaller chunks over the peaches. Bake on the middle rack until crumble begins to brown, about 8 minutes. Drizzle half of the frosting packets from the strudels over the top. Serve.

DUTCH APPLE PIE BITES

These little treats are perfect two-bite desserts...but plan to serve three to four per person, because they are just too easy to pop into your mouth, one after another. You could drizzle a little caramel sauce over the top of each one for an even more indulgent bite. The recipe calls for Granny Smith apples, but you can use any type.

SERVES: 15
PREP TIME: 10 minutes
COOK TIME: 19 minutes
TOTAL TIME: 29 minutes

Ingredients

3½ tablespoons cold salted butter, divided

3 medium Granny Smith apples, peeled, cored, and diced small

½ tablespoon lemon juice

3 tablespoons water

3 tablespoons granulated sugar

¼ teaspoon cinnamon

⅛ teaspoon ground nutmeg

¼ cup all-purpose flour

3 tablespoons brown sugar

½ (1.9-ounce) box frozen phyllo shells (15 shells)

PER SERVING

Calories: 74
Fat: 3g
Protein: 0g
Sodium: 28mg

Fiber: 1g
Carbohydrates: 12g
Sugar: 8g

1. Preheat oven to 400°F.

2. Heat a large skillet over high heat. When hot, add 1½ tablespoons butter and apples. Sauté until apples begin to soften, about 5 minutes. Add lemon juice and water, then cover the skillet to cook for another 3 minutes. Add granulated sugar, cinnamon, and nutmeg. Stir and cook for another 2 minutes. Remove from heat and set aside.

3. While apples cook, in a small bowl, combine flour and brown sugar. Using a pastry cutter or two forks, cut remaining 2 tablespoons butter into dry ingredients until mixture is the size of small peas. Spread mixture on rimmed baking sheet and bake until golden brown, 6–8 minutes. Stir when it comes out of the oven to break up the crumble a bit.

4. Remove shells from packaging and place on baking sheet. Bake for 3 minutes, then fill with apples. Top apples with crumble, pressing into the apples so it sticks. Serve warm.

GRILLED S'MORES

This unique twist on traditional s'mores brings them inside and adds French toast for a special treat. This is how you enjoy s'mores in the dead of winter! If you are feeling adventurous, substitute chocolate peanut butter cups for the chocolate bars.

SERVES: 6
PREP TIME: 5 minutes
COOK TIME: 10 minutes
TOTAL TIME: 15 minutes

Ingredients

3 tablespoons salted butter

12 pieces frozen full-sized slices French toast

3 (1.55-ounce) Hershey's milk chocolate bars

5 full-sized graham crackers, each broken into 4 rectangular pieces

12 regular-sized marshmallows, cut in half

PER SERVING

Calories: 515
Fat: 18g
Protein: 12g
Sodium: 711mg

Fiber: 2g
Carbohydrates: 72g
Sugar: 23g

1. Butter one side of each piece of French toast. Set aside 6 slices French toast. For each s'more, place ½ chocolate bar on the unbuttered side of a piece of French toast. Top with 3 small graham cracker rectangles. Put 4 marshmallow halves on top of graham crackers. Top with a second piece of French toast, buttered side up.

2. Heat a large skillet over medium-low heat. When hot, working in batches if necessary, add s'mores and cover. Allow sandwiches to heat up and brown on first side, about 2–3 minutes. Flip and cover until browned on second side, another 2–3 minutes. Repeat with remaining s'mores. Serve immediately.

COOKIES AND CREAM DESSERT DIP

Dips aren't just for appetizers! This dessert dip is a playful way to serve dessert to a crowd. Get creative with your dipping method—you can use Oreos, strawberries, sliced Granny Smith apples, pretzels, vanilla wafers, or graham crackers. (If you're in a rush, just use a spoon!) Be sure to follow the directions for quick-thawing the frozen whipped topping carefully; otherwise it will melt instead of thaw.

SERVES: 8
PREP TIME: 10 minutes
COOK TIME: N/A
TOTAL TIME: 10 minutes

Ingredients

8 ounces frozen whipped topping

4 ounces cream cheese, softened

½ cup confectioners' sugar

½ teaspoon vanilla extract

20 Oreo cookies

½ cup mini chocolate chips

PER SERVING

Calories: 304
Fat: 16g
Protein: 3g
Sodium: 173mg

Fiber: 1g
Carbohydrates: 36g
Sugar: 23g

1. Dump whipped topping into a medium microwave-safe bowl. Microwave at 30 percent power in 30-second increments until thawed, about 3–4 times.

2. In a separate medium bowl, beat together cream cheese, confectioners' sugar, and vanilla until smooth. Fold in the thawed whipped topping.

3. Put Oreos in a large plastic zipper bag and close. Use a rolling pin to crush them (it's okay to leave a few larger pieces). Add crumbs to the bowl, along with the chocolate chips, and mix well. Serve with the dipping items.

MILE-HIGH CHOCOLATE CREAM PIE

This rich chocolate treat is a cinch to make but will taste like you spent an afternoon putting it together. To kick it up a notch, top the pie with fun additions like Oreo pieces, toffee bits, chopped Andes creme de menthe thins, or fresh berries.

SERVES: 8
PREP TIME: 20 minutes
COOK TIME: 10 minutes
TOTAL TIME: 30 minutes

Ingredients

1 (9") frozen piecrust shell

2 cups cold 1% milk

2 (3.4-ounce) boxes instant chocolate pudding

2 cups cold heavy cream

1 (7-ounce) can whipped cream topping

PER SERVING

Calories: 493
Fat: 32g
Protein: 5g
Sodium: 565mg

Fiber: 2g
Carbohydrates: 42g
Sugar: 27g

1. Preheat oven to 400°F. Unwrap piecrust and set on the stovetop to begin to defrost while oven preheats.

2. Use a fork to poke holes around the surface of the crust. Bake crust until lightly browned, about 10 minutes. Remove from the oven and place in the freezer for 6–7 minutes to cool down.

3. While crust is baking, prepare filling by combining milk and pudding mix with an electric hand mixer on low speed until completely smooth, about 2 minutes. Add heavy cream and beat on high speed until mixture becomes thick, about 2 minutes. Spoon filling into cooled piecrust, top with a dollop of whipped cream, and serve.

CINNAMON PRETZEL BITES WITH SALTED CARAMEL DIP

These soft pretzels are reminiscent of the popular mall store's offerings, made in the comfort of your own home. Don't be intimidated by the homemade caramel dip—it is extremely simple to make. If you have any leftover caramel, you can store it safely in the refrigerator for 3 months. Just reheat it in the microwave for an ice cream topping or as a dip for apple slices.

SERVES: 4
PREP TIME: 10 minutes
COOK TIME: 20 minutes
TOTAL TIME: 30 minutes

Ingredients

1½ cups granulated sugar, divided

1½ teaspoons light corn syrup

⅛ teaspoon cream of tartar

½ cup water

½ cup heavy cream

¼ teaspoon kosher salt

4 frozen unsalted soft pretzels

4 tablespoons salted butter, melted

2 teaspoons cinnamon

PER SERVING

Calories: 665
Fat: 21g
Protein: 5g
Sodium: 350mg

Fiber: 2g
Carbohydrates: 113g
Sugar: 79g

1. Preheat oven to 400°F. Grease a rimmed cookie sheet with nonstick spray.

2. In a medium saucepan, combine 1 cup sugar, corn syrup, cream of tartar, and water. Place over high heat and do not stir. Cook until mixture reaches 230°F on a candy thermometer, then reduce heat to medium. Once mixture reaches 300°F, stir well, then allow it to come to 330°F. Turn off heat and add cream and salt. Mix well, return to medium heat, and cook for another 2 minutes. Transfer caramel into a heatproof bowl and allow it to begin cooling.

3. On a microwave-safe plate, microwave frozen pretzels on high for 45 seconds. Cut each pretzel into 2" pieces. In a medium bowl, toss pretzel pieces in melted butter to coat.

4. In a medium bowl, combine remaining ½ cup sugar with cinnamon. Add pretzel pieces and toss to coat them in the cinnamon sugar. Place on prepared baking sheet and bake for 7 minutes. Serve with caramel dip.

ORANGE CREAMSICLE TRUFFLES

There are only five ingredients in these refreshing little bites of creamy citrus goodness. This is a great recipe to make with kids. They will love helping to form each ball in their hands then rolling it around in the cookie crumbs. If you like coconut, you could add ½ cup to the food processor when you are pulsing the second batch of cookies to give them a bit of a tropical touch.

SERVES: 6 (makes 30 truffles)
PREP TIME: 30 minutes
COOK TIME: N/A
TOTAL TIME: 30 minutes

Ingredients

1 (11-ounce) package pecan sandies cookies, divided

2 ounces cream cheese, softened

¼ cup frozen orange juice concentrate

Zest of ½ medium orange

1¾ cups confectioners' sugar

PER SERVING

Calories: 443
Fat: 18g
Protein: 3g
Sodium: 219mg

Fiber: 1g
Carbohydrates: 64g
Sugar: 44g

1. In a food processor, process half the cookies into crumbs. Pour onto a plate and set aside.

2. Process remaining cookies into crumbs. Add cream cheese, frozen concentrate, and orange zest. Pulse to combine, then add confectioners' sugar. Pulse until the mixture comes together into a dough. Spread dough onto a plate and freeze for 15 minutes to firm up.

3. For each truffle, form a ball with about 1 tablespoon cold dough. Roll the ball in reserved cookie crumbs. Serve immediately. Refrigerate any leftover truffles for up to 1 week.

US/Metric Conversion Chart

VOLUME CONVERSIONS

US Volume Measure	Metric Equivalent
⅛ teaspoon	0.5 milliliter
¼ teaspoon	1 milliliter
½ teaspoon	2 milliliters
1 teaspoon	5 milliliters
½ tablespoon	7 milliliters
1 tablespoon (3 teaspoons)	15 milliliters
2 tablespoons (1 fluid ounce)	30 milliliters
¼ cup (4 tablespoons)	60 milliliters
⅓ cup	90 milliliters
½ cup (4 fluid ounces)	125 milliliters
⅔ cup	160 milliliters
¾ cup (6 fluid ounces)	180 milliliters
1 cup (16 tablespoons)	250 milliliters
1 pint (2 cups)	500 milliliters
1 quart (4 cups)	1 liter (about)

WEIGHT CONVERSIONS

US Weight Measure	Metric Equivalent
½ ounce	15 grams
1 ounce	30 grams
2 ounces	60 grams
3 ounces	85 grams
¼ pound (4 ounces)	115 grams
½ pound (8 ounces)	225 grams
¾ pound (12 ounces)	340 grams
1 pound (16 ounces)	454 grams

OVEN TEMPERATURE CONVERSIONS

Degrees Fahrenheit	Degrees Celsius
200 degrees F	95 degrees C
250 degrees F	120 degrees C
275 degrees F	135 degrees C
300 degrees F	150 degrees C
325 degrees F	160 degrees C
350 degrees F	180 degrees C
375 degrees F	190 degrees C
400 degrees F	205 degrees C
425 degrees F	220 degrees C
450 degrees F	230 degrees C

BAKING PAN SIZES

American	Metric
8 x 1½ inch round baking pan	20 x 4 cm cake tin
9 x 1½ inch round baking pan	23 x 3.5 cm cake tin
11 x 7 x 1½ inch baking pan	28 x 18 x 4 cm baking tin
13 x 9 x 2 inch baking pan	30 x 20 x 5 cm baking tin
2 quart rectangular baking dish	30 x 20 x 3 cm baking tin
15 x 10 x 2 inch baking pan	30 x 25 x 2 cm baking tin (Swiss roll tin)
9 inch pie plate	22 x 4 or 23 x 4 cm pie plate
7 or 8 inch springform pan	18 or 20 cm spring-form or loose bottom cake tin
9 x 5 x 3 inch loaf pan	23 x 13 x 7 cm or 2 lb narrow loaf or pâté tin
1½ quart casserole	1.5 liter casserole
2 quart casserole	2 liter casserole

Index

About the Author

Carole Jones is a Minnesota-based food blogger, recipe creator, and author of the *Take 5: Chicken* e-cookbook. For the past twelve years, she has shared her culinary adventures cooking and baking for her six brutally honest children at MyKitchenEscapades.com. Hot, crusty bread is Carole's love language, but her two adorable grandchildren are a close second. Yes, second. Don't judge.

Carole's recipes have been featured by *Good Housekeeping*, *FamilyFun Magazine*, Pillsbury, *The Kitchn*, *Lifehacker*, *BuzzFeed*, and Michaels stores. She has also partnered to create content with Disney, Wolf Gourmet, Campbell's, Land O'Lakes, Del Monte, Tyson, Heinz, and Marzetti. In 2013, she founded Breaking Bread, an innovative food-based leadership development program that utilizes cooking to cultivate employee engagement.